GROW

MATURING BELIEVERS THROUGH *the* TRUTHS *of the* CHRISTIAN FAITH

BY RUSSELL A. BOARD

Published by
LIFESPRINGS RESOURCES
FRANKLIN SPRINGS, GA

CONTENTS

How to Use This Book 4

Introduction 5

Chapter One: *God's Message* 7

Chapter Two: *God Is* 15

Chapter Three: *God Speaks* 23

Chapter Four: *God Comes* 31

Chapter Five: *God Dwells* 37

Chapter Six: *God Transforms* 45

Chapter Seven: *God Listens* 53

Chapter Eight: *God Gathers* 61

Chapter Nine: *God Reminds* 69

Chapter Ten: *God Is Worthy* 75

Chapter Eleven: *God Gives* 83

Chapter Twelve: *God Sends* 91

Chapter Thirteen: *God Returns* 99

HOW TO USE THIS BOOK

As the introduction states, this book is primarily meant for new believers, as well as mature believers who may be looking for a refresher course concerning the building blocks of the Christian faith. However, it may also be used to introduce anyone unfamiliar with Christianity to some of its core beliefs and practices.

So how should this book be used? The best way to answer this question is to mention some settings in which it may be fruitfully used. First, any individual person can pick up and read this book for their personal study and edification. It can be read from cover to cover, beginning with chapter one and read right through to the end of the book. Or you may have a particular question about a certain Christian teaching (these teachings are called doctrines). If so, just flip to the chapter that will best answer your question and start reading.

Second, this book may be used in one-on-one discipleship. A more mature believer can walk a new believer through this book, working through the questions and exercises at the end of each chapter and answering any other questions the new Christian might have.

Third, this book would be a fine tool to use in a small group Bible study. The reflection questions at the end of each chapter can be used to foster discussion. Many of us learn better when we're able to discuss what we've read with others.

Fourth, this book may also be used in a Sunday school or other formal teaching setting. For those who go this route, you may want to utilize the companion Leader's Guide. It includes lesson plans, teaching suggestions, and additional resources that correspond to each chapter. The Leader's Guide and additional resources may be downloaded for free from www.lifesprings.net/grow.html.

One final word to those who may not be familiar with how biblical citations should be read. The Bible includes 66 books. These books contain chapters and verses. Biblical citations are a short way to tell you where a biblical quote or biblical idea can be found. The title of a book is listed first, followed by the chapter, and then the verse or verses. A colon separates chapter and verse(s). They look something like this: Matthew 28:18-20. This citation refers to a passage of Scripture in the book of Matthew, Chapter 28, and verses 18 through 20.

However you choose to use this book, may it foster a love and joy for Scripture and the God it reveals.

Introduction

I haven't been blessed with what is called a "green thumb." It seems that any time I get a plant or flower, it doesn't survive more than a week or two. But rather than resulting from some flaw in my genetic makeup, my failures are mainly due to a lack of attention to the essential conditions necessary for vegetation to thrive. I fail to put the plant in a place where it gets enough sunlight, or I fail to water it properly. Neglecting these necessities inevitably leads to a withered, fruitless plant.

Christians also need proper spiritual nourishment if they are not only to survive, but also to thrive. In fact, the Bible actually uses the metaphor of a flourishing, fruitful tree to describe a person who is rooted and grounded in the word of God (see Psalm 1:1-6).

The lessons in this study cover basic truths that every believer needs to know in order to live a life that is pleasing to the Lord. The content of these lessons will help to supply fertile soil and essential nutrients for Christian growth and discipleship.

If you are a new Christian, these studies will help to get you started in the right direction in your walk with God. With these truths planted in your heart and mind, you will be well equipped to live a faithful and fruitful Christian life.

But this study is not just for new Christians. Even if you have been a Christian for many years, it is a good idea to "get back to the basics" from time to time and review the fundamentals. These lessons can serve to remind you of truths you may have forgotten, fill in the gaps in areas you may have missed, and clarify concepts that may still be unclear.

May these lessons equip you to "live a life worthy of the calling you have received," and help you to "grow to become in every respect the mature body of him who is the head, that is, Christ" (Ephesians 4:1, 15).

CHAPTER ONE:

God's Message

Jesus is called *Savior* because He came "to seek and to save the lost" (Luke 19:10). The concept of salvation is fundamental to Christianity. In this chapter, we examine what it means to be saved.

WHO NEEDS TO BE SAVED?

Everyone! The Bible makes it clear that the entire human race is in need of Jesus Christ to provide salvation. There are no exceptions. This is because we are all infected by what the Bible calls "sin." This infection has progressed to different degrees in different people, so that there are obvious differences in moral character from person to person. Nevertheless, the infection is present in all of us, and it is deadly. We are all sinners (Romans 3:10-18, 23).

WHAT IS SIN?

In the beginning, when God created the universe, everything He made was good (Genesis 1). God designed all things to operate according to the laws He established.

The third chapter of Genesis tells the story of how the first man and woman broke the law of God, with disastrous results. At that point, God's perfect creation was marred, and though it still shows the glory of its Creator, it has never been the same. Since that time, pain and sorrow, suffering and death have plagued the world. And the actions of every human being born into the world since (with the exception of Jesus Christ) have shown an inborn tendency to rebel against God's law. This is what we mean by "sin."

Sin is not a small matter. To sin is not just to make a minor mistake, or to break what appears to be one of society's arbitrary rules. To sin is to set oneself in opposition to God and to transgress against the very foundations upon which the universe is built. When we sin, we attempt to make ourselves the ultimate lawgivers, and we substitute our own self-made laws for the laws of God. We thereby wreck the design of God both for our own individual lives and for the world we live in.

Sin can be defined simply as "doing as you please" (cf. Isaiah 53:6). This may sound innocent enough until we realize that it is, in reality, a rejection of God's authority over His creation. When we sin, we rebel against the One who created and sustains our lives, and we claim for ourselves the right to determine how to run things. Every sin is an act of defiance, an attempt to push God off His throne and take His place.

Sin also includes the failure to do what we ought to do (James 4:17). Sin is failing to recognize the authority of God and to offer Him the worship, thanks, and obedience that are His due (Romans 1:18-21). Sin is failing to live up to our responsibilities as sons and daughters, husbands and wives, fathers and mothers, and stewards of God's creation. Sin is failing to love God and others (Matthew 22:37-39).

Sin has its root in pride and selfishness. These things are, first of all, inward conditions. They eventually result in outward actions, but the source of the problem is located inside us, in what we are, not just in what we do (Matthew 5:21, 22, 27, 28). We sin because we are, by nature, sinners.

WHAT ARE THE RESULTS OF SIN?

Because of sin, all of humanity is under the wrath of God, deserving of punishment for breaking His laws. We are all guilty before Him, and we stand condemned with no excuse to offer (Ephesians 2:1-3). As condemned sinners, we face a destiny of eternal punishment in hell, the place God has set aside for those who refuse to submit to His authority.

God warned Adam and Eve that disobedience to His law would result in death. More than the decay and eventual mortality that afflicts our physical bodies, this refers to the spiritual death that now afflicts the soul of every person born into the world.

God created us to have communion with Him, to know and fellowship with Him. But sin brought separation from God, as our rebellion cut us off from Him. Because of sin, the spirit of humanity (that part of it which relates to and communes with God) is dead, and humanity has lost the consciousness of God's presence. In this state of spiritual death, we cannot see, know, or please God.

Sin is deceitful; we are fooled into thinking we will find freedom in rejecting the law of God and becoming our own boss. But in fact, sin robs us of freedom and puts us in bondage (John 8:34). We find ourselves trapped, unable to free ourselves from sin's power and unable to do what we know is right (Romans 7:18, 19).

Thus the natural state of sinful humanity is an unhappy one: guilty, spiritually dead, and enslaved to sin. Moreover, sin is never a private matter; its repercussions spill over into the family (broken relationships, divorce), into society (crime, injustice), and into the natural world (pollution, waste).

WHAT CAN WE DO TO SAVE OURSELVES FROM SIN'S RESULTS?

How can those who are morally defiled cleanse the stain of sin from their souls? How can slaves tear off their chains of bondage? How can the dead bring themselves back to life?

The truth is it is impossible for us to save ourselves. There is nothing we can do to remove the guilt of our sin. We cannot undo the sins we have committed; what's done is done, and the past cannot be changed. So even if we were never to commit another sin in the future, the sins of the past would remain to condemn us.

Worse still, the problem goes deeper than the evil acts themselves. Remember that sin is first an inward condition, a problem that afflicts our very nature. The infection in our heart needs to be cured. This is beyond our ability (Jeremiah 13:23). We need help.

WHAT DID GOD DO ABOUT OUR CONDITION?

Thank God, He did not leave us in this hopeless state. Two thousand years ago, Jesus Christ, God's own Son, took upon Himself the punishment for our sins when He suffered and died on a Roman cross. Though Jesus was divine, He suffered death as any other person would; though He was righteous and innocent, He was punished in our place (Isaiah 53:4-6). After three days, He was raised from the dead in victory over sin and death, having broken the bonds that held us captive (Acts 2:24).

God did this in order to reunite us with Himself, to restore the relationship that our sin had broken. God did not and could not overlook our sin, but He paid the price to make amends for it and redeem us from its curse (Ephesians 1:7).

God became a human being in order to do what we could not do for ourselves. He came to earth and died in order to bring us back to Himself (2 Corinthians 5:19-21). His resurrection proved and sealed His defeat of sin and its penalty, death. Through grace God provided a remedy for our desperate predicament.

WHAT IS GRACE?

We are saved by God's grace. This means that salvation is *all* God's doing. We are not saved because we deserve it, are worthy of it, or do something to earn it. There is nothing in us that deserves the salvation God offers us; it is a free gift that flows to us from God's unfathomable love. Our attempts to be or to do good can add nothing to what Christ has already done. He is the Savior, and He alone saves (Ephesians 2:8, 9).

HOW DO WE RECEIVE THE SALVATION GOD HAS PROVIDED FOR US IN CHRIST?

Even though God has done everything necessary to provide for our salvation, it does not come to us automatically. We must receive the gift God offers. How do we do this?

1. **Repent.** In order to receive salvation in Christ, we must first recognize our need for it. This means confessing our sinful condition and turning from it to seek God's forgiveness.

2. **Believe.** We must believe that this forgiveness is ours in Christ, and trust in Him alone to save us.
3. **Submit.** We must put our lives in His hands and give Him complete control, for only then can He save us. Jesus is both Savior and Lord.

A simple prayer is all that is necessary to call upon the name of the Lord and receive the salvation that is ours in Christ (Romans 10:9-13).

WHAT HAPPENS WHEN WE TRUST CHRIST ALONE FOR OUR SALVATION?

God made the first move when Christ became man to die for our sins. He makes the next move, as well, when He causes us to hear and understand the gospel of salvation and draws us to Himself by His Holy Spirit (John 6:44). When we respond to His call in repentance and faith, believing and receiving this gospel, God moves again. When God saves us, several things happen:

- **We are regenerated** (Ephesians 2:1; 2 Corinthians 5:17). Our spirits, which were dead because of sin, are given a new birth through the Holy Spirit of God (John 3:3-8). We become spiritually alive, and our communion with God is restored. The heart that was infected with sin is cleansed and made new. We are united with Christ and given new life, eternal life, His life in us.

- **We are justified** (Romans 3:23-26). This means that we are declared innocent in God's sight. Christ has taken our sin upon Himself, and in return we are clothed with His righteousness (2 Corinthians 5:21). All of our sin is removed from us and forgotten (Psalm 103:12; Isaiah 43:25), and we stand before God blameless.

- **We are adopted into God's family** (Romans 8:14-17). With our new birth, we are reborn into the family of God. He takes us to Himself and makes us His children. We have a new relationship with God, and we can truly call Him "Father," as His Holy Spirit comes to live within us and mark us as His possessions (Ephesians 1:13, 14). How great is God's grace, which goes even beyond justifying and cleansing us to make us His very own children (1 John 3:1).

FOR WHAT PURPOSE ARE WE SAVED?

When we receive God's gift of salvation in Christ, it is only the first step in a never-ending journey with God. God saves us for a purpose, in order that we may love, serve, and glorify Him throughout our lives—in this world and through all eternity (Ephesians 2:10; John 17:24).

God's ultimate goal is that we become like Christ, conformed to His image (Romans 8:29). God is at work in you and in me to make us more and more like Jesus. Everything that He does in us and for us, everything He brings into our lives, has this glorious end in view. And we can be confident that God will complete this marvelous work He has begun in us, for His own glory (Philippians 1:6).

REFLECT & RESPOND

1. Why is it necessary for someone to be saved in order to have fellowship with God?

2. Can a person do anything to save himself or herself? What are some of the ways people try to save themselves? Why don't these attempts work?

3. What happens when we trust Christ alone for our salvation?

Q&A
Read Ephesians 2:1-10.

1. How does Paul describe our lives before God saved us?

2. What did God do for us? Why?

3. How are we saved?

4. What is faith?

5. What is God's purpose for our lives?

FOR FURTHER STUDY

Gilbert, Greg. *What Is the Gospel?* Wheaton, IL: Crossway Books, 2010.

Stott, John R. W. *The Cross of Christ.* Downers Grove, IL: InterVarsity Press, 2006.

Tchividjian, Tullian. *Jesus + Nothing = Everything.* Wheaton, IL: Crossway Books, 2011.

CHAPTER TWO:
God Is

The study of God is called *theology*. Many people think of theology as a difficult, boring, and impractical subject that only scholars or seminarians should study. Is this true?

Certainly, the study of God can be difficult. Indeed, it is impossible for us, with our finite intelligence, even to begin to know God. But God has not left us on our own, to grope for answers in the dark. He has shown us what He is like because He wants us to know Him. God's revelation of Himself to us is what makes theology possible.

The study of God is anything but boring. What could be more exciting than to learn about the One who created the world and those who live in it? Indeed, the reason so many people lead aimless, empty lives is that they do not know God, the source of life, and so they do not know what life is all about. If we do not know God, then we cannot truly know ourselves or the purpose of our existence.

Impractical? On the contrary, theology is essential because knowing God is essential.

HOW DOES GOD REVEAL HIMSELF?

God makes Himself known to us in several ways:

Creation

Looking at the world God has made can help us learn about Him. This is sometimes called *general revelation* because it is given in a general way to the whole world. The vast, magnificent universe bears witness to the wisdom, power, and glory of God, its Creator (Psalm 19:1-4; Romans 1:19, 20). We ourselves, created in God's image (Genesis 1:27), have minds that reflect His intelligence and consciences that attest to His justice. God's general revelation is inescapable. Every time we open our eyes we are presented with His handiwork; every time we take a breath we are reminded of His faithfulness in sustaining our lives.

Scripture

The knowledge of God we can obtain from creation is limited, but God has given us *special revelation* of Himself in the Bible. This is the normal means God has ordained to make Himself known to us. Through the Holy Spirit, God inspired the authors of Scripture to record particular words and deeds about Himself, giving us a more complete picture of what He is like (2 Timothy 3:16; 2 Peter 1:21). The Bible contains accounts of God's dealings with humanity, truths godly people have learned from and about Him, and messages spoken directly from God to us. In all of this, God tells us about Himself.

Special Visitations

The Bible describes how God has sometimes appeared to people in dreams, visions, and other extraordinary experiences. These were invariably powerful and life-changing events (see Exodus 3:1-6; Isaiah 6:1-8; Acts 9:1-8). God may still choose to meet or speak to people in such ways, although these are not His normal means of making Himself known.

Jesus Christ

The fullest and most complete revelation of God is found in Jesus Christ (Hebrews 1:1-3). Jesus is called the Word because He is the perfect expression of what God reveals to us of Himself (John 1:1). In Christ, God took human form in order that we might look upon the invisible God (John 1:14; Colossians 1:15). In Christ, God spoke with a human voice and had a tangible body that could be seen, heard, and touched (1 John 1:1, 2). If we want to see God, we need only look at Jesus (John 14:7-10).

The Holy Spirit

Our most direct and personal knowledge of God comes from the Holy Spirit, who comes to live within us. Through the Holy Spirit, God draws near to us and makes Himself known to our hearts (John 14:15-23). What a precious privilege, to know God in such a close and intimate way!

God's People

We should also note that God created humankind in order to reflect His image (Genesis 1:26, 27), and He chose Abraham and his descendants to testify to the rest of the world about what He is like (Genesis 12:1-3). Of course, sin and disobedience have marred the human reflection of God and tarnished the testimony of His people. Now it is the church which has been called to show the world what God is like (Matthew 5:16, 48). As the body of Christ (1 Corinthians 12:27), we are sent to tell others about the Father, and His Son, Jesus Christ (John 20:21). God makes Himself known through the attitudes and actions of His people in conjunction with His people sharing the gospel (1 Thessalonians 1:7-10).

IS THERE MORE THAN ONE GOD?

There is only one true God, Creator of heaven and earth (Deuteronomy 4:39; Isaiah 45:18). He alone is worthy of our worship. To be sure, there are other spiritual beings with powers and modes of existence beyond our own (i.e., angels and demons). But these are also created beings subject to and dependent upon the one and only God. All other so-called "gods" are false, either dumb idols or demonic impostors (1 Corinthians 8:4-6; 10:20).

The one and only God exists in three persons, in what the Church has historically called the *Trinity*. The three persons of the Trinity are one in substance, nature, and purpose. They have existed from all eternity in a state of perfect harmony and love. God's personality is the foundation and model of human personality; the interrelationship within the Trinity is the foundation and model for all human relationships.

One must remember the Bible declares this *one* God is a tri-unity. He is not three gods, or three parts of God, but one God in three distinct persons.

WHO ARE THE PERSONS OF THE TRINITY?

The Trinity is God the Father, God the Son, and God the Holy Spirit (Matthew 3:16, 17; 28:19). All are divine and co-equal. Their relationships to one another and the roles they adopt in relation to us make them distinguishable.

God the Father created the universe through the agency of God the Son by the power of God the Holy Spirit. Similarly, God the Father redeemed His creation through the agency of God the Son by the power of God the Holy Spirit.

God the Son has existed eternally in a loving and submissive relationship with God the Father (John 1:1; 8:28, 29). Through the power of the Holy Spirit, God the Son became incarnate ("in flesh") as the man Jesus Christ, fully divine and fully human. He lived in perfect obedience to the Father, and He worked miracles through the power of the Holy Spirit. He died in our place to make amends (atone) for our sins; the Father raised Him through the Holy Spirit and now reigns as King over all. From His throne at the right hand of the Father, He gives the Holy Spirit to His people (Acts 2:32, 33).

God the Holy Spirit is now continually at work in the world, convicting people of sin (John 16:8) and drawing them back to the Father through the Son. He glorifies the Son and leads people to faith in Him (John 16:14). He applies the salvation the Son purchased, giving new life to those who believe in Him (John 3:3, 8). The Father sends the Spirit into our hearts to testify that we are His children (Galatians 4:6). The Holy Spirit lives within believers, filling them with the power and love of God (Romans 5:5; 8:11).

WHAT IS GOD LIKE?

47,000
17,000
17,000

God is eternal.

The first words of the Bible are "In the beginning God" (Genesis 1:1). Before the universe existed, before there was anything else, there was God (Psalm 90:2). The cosmos did not cause its own existence (a logical and metaphysical impossibility); the eternally existing God brought into being matter, space, and time. He alone is independent and uncreated (Acts 17:24, 25). He was, He is, and He always will be (Revelation 4:8). God is the great I AM (Exodus 3:14), the self-existing One. If God did not exist, nothing else would or could. He is the ultimate reality that grounds the existence of everything else.

God is infinite.

God is Spirit, not subject to the limitations of a material body (John 4:24). He is infinite in presence (omnipresent), not confined to one location (Jeremiah 23:24; Psalm 139:7-10). He is infinite in knowledge (omniscient), so that nothing is hidden or unknown to Him (Psalm 94:7-11). He is infinite in power (omnipotent), so there is nothing too difficult for Him (Jeremiah 32:27).

God is sovereign.

God brought the universe into being out of nothing (Genesis 1:1). The universe is not a manifestation or a part of God, but a separate creation, dependent upon God for its continued existence (Colossians 1:17). God reigns over His creation, and nothing in it is outside of His control. He did not create it and then leave it to run on its own. He is not an absentee landlord. It is He who determines the course of history, and though He grants a measure of freedom to His creatures, He maintains ultimate control over all that happens (Psalm 135:6). In fact, He has entered history at a point in time through His Son. His moral will may not always be done, but He uses even the disobedience of people and angels to the service of His plans. His purposes cannot be frustrated (Daniel 4:35).

God is personal.

God is not some cosmic "force" that permeates and energizes the universe, which we can manipulate or use for our purposes. He is not a vague "influence," but a person, who thinks, feels, speaks, plans, and acts. He is not less personal than we are, but more so (Psalm 94:7-10). He has a distinct character and will; He can be pleased or offended, known or ignored, obeyed or disobeyed, loved or despised.

God is holy (Isaiah 6:3).

Holiness entails perfection, purity, majesty, and glory. God is perfectly righteous and pure, which means He does not, cannot, and never will sin (James 1:13; 1 John 1:5). He is supreme in value and worth. He lives in unapproachable light (1 Timothy 6:16), and He is the source and ideal of all goodness and truth. His judgments are in accord with perfect justice. There is none like Him in all of heaven and earth (1 Samuel 2:2).

God is love (1 John 4:8).

Every instance of human love we experience or witness—the love of a mother for her child, the love between husband and wife, the love which binds two people in friendship—is but a pale imitation of the love which overflows from the heart of God. God's love is abundant enough to envelop the vilest sinner and redeem him back to Himself. Christ's sacrifice for us on the cross of Calvary measures the depth of God's love (John 3:16; Romans 5:8; 1 John 4:10). Who can comprehend such love as this? Who can refuse it?

REFLECT & RESPOND

1. What is the most difficult truth about God for you to understand or believe? Why? What is the easiest? Why?

2. What is unique about the God of the Bible compared to all other gods?

3. What are some of the gods you're drawn to, rather than the one true God? Why do you think that is?

Q&A
Read Jeremiah 10:1-16.
1. How is the one true God different from false gods made with human hands?

Read Jeremiah 9:23, 24.
2. What is more valuable than wisdom, power, and wealth?

3. What does God delight in?

4. How can we know God better?

FOR FURTHER STUDY

Carson, D. A. *The God Who Is There: Finding Your Place in God's Story.* Grand Rapids, MI: Baker Books, 2010.

Packer, J. I. *Knowing God.* Downers Grove, IL: InterVarsity Press, 1993.

Tozer, A. W. *The Knowledge of the Holy: The Attributes of God: Their Meaning in the Christian Life.* New York, NY: HarperOne, 1978.

CHAPTER THREE:
God Speaks

WHAT IS THE BIBLE?

The Bible is the Word of God; therefore, it is the supreme authority for all Christians. No person, organization, or government possesses authority greater than that of the Bible. In any question of doctrine or practice, in any dispute over what to believe or how to behave, the Bible's answer is final. Every individual and every institution is required to submit to the authority of Scripture.

The Bible is authoritative because it came from God. It is God's written communication to humanity. Therefore, the Bible is infallible; since God is its author, it is completely trustworthy. Everything the Bible affirms is true. We can have complete confidence in the Bible, and we are called to give complete obedience to it.

HOW WAS THE BIBLE WRITTEN?

Except for the tablets of stone given to Moses on Mount Sinai (see Exodus 31:18), God did not write the Bible directly. Rather, we are told some human beings "spoke from God as they were carried along by the Spirit" (2 Peter 1:21). God used people to record His words to us.

Some forty different men, over a period of about 1600 years, wrote the Bible we have today. Yet the 66 books fit together to present one complete and consistent revelation of God. The scriptures are said to be

"God-breathed" (2 Timothy 3:16). This means that through the Holy Spirit God directed certain individuals to write what He wanted written. This is not to say that God dictated the words in a mechanical way; rather, He allowed the writers to say what they wanted to say, to express themselves in their own words and writing styles. Yet God created and chose these persons, and He sovereignly directed their lives to prepare them to be His instruments. Then His Holy Spirit enabled and led them to write precisely what He wanted them to write, word for word. This is sometimes referred to as the inspiration of Scripture.

HOW DO WE KNOW THE BIBLE IS THE WORD OF GOD?

There are many good reasons to believe in the authority and inspiration of Scripture:

The Bible claims for itself divine authority.

Time after time, the prophets whose words are recorded claimed to be delivering the "word of the Lord." Those who heard them often rejected the message and sometimes reacted violently, even killing the divine messengers. The blood of the prophets attests to the truth of their words. The apostles of Christ testified to the authority and inspiration of Scripture (Romans 15:4; 2 Timothy 3:16; 2 Peter 1:21).

Jesus believed the Bible is God's Word.

Jesus Christ, the Son of God, testified to the infallibility (trustworthiness and accuracy) and eternal truth of the scriptures as the written Word of God (John 10:35; Matthew 5:17,18; Matthew 4:4; John 17:17).

The Bible records the fulfillment of prophecy.

Scores of prophetic predictions recorded in the scriptures have been fulfilled in history, thus confirming their divine authorship.

Archaeological finds affirm the truthfulness of the Bible.

Archaeological discoveries continue to confirm the Bible's descriptions of ancient life and history.

Over 2,000 years of church history affirms the Bible as the Word of God.

Throughout its history, the Church has affirmed that the Bible is the inspired Word of God. The holy and victorious lives of the saints through the ages demonstrate that the Bible is a true and sure foundation for living.

The content of the Bible points to one source, a primary author.

The unified message, enduring wisdom, and sublime beauty of Scripture point to a source beyond the diverse and often unlearned persons who wrote it. This source is God.

The Bible is self-authenticating.

Finally, the Bible proves itself to be the Word of God in our own experience. It reveals the secrets of our hearts as only God can, and when we obey it, we find that God keeps the promises recorded therein. We can hear God's voice speaking directly to us in the words of the Bible, and discover for ourselves the truth of what is written there.

HOW DID WE COME TO HAVE THE BIBLE WE USE TODAY?

The Bible we use has been translated from the original languages in which it was written, mostly Hebrew in the Old Testament, with some Aramaic, and Greek in the New Testament. The original works (autographs) the biblical writers penned no longer exist, but there are literally thousands of handwritten copies dating from the first centuries after Christ. It is from these, together with other early translations of Scripture, that scholars who are experts in ancient history and languages translated the Bible. We can have confidence that the Bible we have today is a faithful and accurate translation of what the inspired authors first wrote.

WHAT ABOUT THE DIFFERENT ENGLISH VERSIONS OF THE BIBLE?

In the medieval era, only priests and scholars who read Latin could read the Bible for themselves, and the lack of printing technology meant that few people could own a copy. In the fourteenth century, people such as John Wycliffe and William Tyndale were persecuted for trying to make God's Word accessible in the language of the common people. In 1611 the King James Version of the Bible was completed; it remains quite popular, even though its sometimes archaic language can be difficult for modern readers. In the twentieth century, several new versions have been published which employ more modern and familiar English. These translations also make use of recently discovered ancient manuscripts, which were unknown in the days the King James Version was produced.

Which translation of the Bible should you use? The beauty of the King James Version is unsurpassed, but it is of little benefit if the words cannot be understood. A paraphrased version (such as the New Living Translation or The Message) can be helpful, but a paraphrase reflects the interpretation of the translator, so it should not be a substitute for a more faithful translation. The New International Version has become the most popular recent translation because it is accurate and easily understood. The English Standard Version is accurate and straightforward, and it is now in widespread use. Many people find it helpful to use a version they can easily understand for daily reading, while keeping other translations and paraphrases on hand for purposes of comparison and study.

WHAT IS THE BIBLE?

The Old Testament (Hebrew Scripture) contains the Scripture Jesus and His Jewish contemporaries used. It includes:

1. **Books of history** recounting the story of early humanity and of God's chosen people, Israel, and revealing God's laws (Genesis through Esther).
2. **Books of wisdom and poetry** expressing truths about life in this world and how we relate to the God who created it (Job through Song of Solomon).
3. **Books of prophecy** recording the warnings and exhortations of prophets called to deliver the messages of God to His often stubborn and disobedient people (Isaiah through Malachi).

The New Testament contains the Scripture that the apostles or their associates wrote immediately after the time of Jesus. It includes:

1. **Four Gospels** that record the words and deeds of Jesus (Matthew through John).
2. A **book of history** describing the formation and growth of the early church (Acts).
3. **Letters** to churches and individuals explaining the Christian faith (doctrine) and giving instructions on how to faithfully live the Christian life (Romans through Jude).
4. One final **vision** given to the apostle John describing the triumph of Christ and His people over Satan and all other enemies (Revelation).

Together the two Testaments constitute the greatest literary masterpiece ever written, giving us the whole counsel of God expressed in a variety of literary forms.

WHAT IS THE MESSAGE OF THE BIBLE?

The Bible deals with the fundamental issues that confront us all: questions of meaning and purpose, right and wrong, life and death. In it God tells us about Himself, about the world He created, about humanity, about Christ, and about salvation. The Bible does not tell us everything we would like to know, but it does tell us everything we need to know concerning our relationship to God and our life with Him.

As the Bible is the written Word of God, so Jesus Christ is the living Word (John 1:1, 14). Thus, from Genesis to Revelation, the central theme of the Bible is Christ (Luke 24:27). He is the link that connects all the very different books, and He is the key to understanding everything that is contained in them. The Old Testament points forward to Christ, predicting His coming, describing His kingdom, and picturing the salvation He brings. The New Testament, in turn, completes the Old, revealing Jesus Christ as the fulfillment of all God's purposes.

WHY SHOULD WE STUDY THE BIBLE?

Though we are able to learn something about God through the world He made (Romans 1:20), we could know nothing of the salvation provided for us in Christ without God's special revelation of Himself in His Word. In order for us to know God, God must reveal Himself to us, and He has revealed Himself in the Bible. If we desire to know Christ, the living Word, we can learn of Him in the scriptures, the written Word.

The Bible tells us who Christ is, who we are in Christ, and what God expects of us. It is full of promises and warnings that are essential to our well-being as Christians (2 Timothy 3:16, 17; 1 Peter 2:2). It helps us to resist temptation (Luke 4:1-12), and it keeps us from sinning (Psalm 119:9-11). We are commanded to be transformed by the renewing of our minds (Romans 12:2), and our minds are renewed as we study the Bible. We then begin to lose the world's perspective and to see things as God sees them, to think with the mind of Christ (1 Corinthians 2:16).

Moreover, the Christian who wants to hear God speaking to him or her individually and personally will turn to the Bible, for the Spirit of God can illuminate a verse or passage that was written in the distant past and apply it to our present situation. Indeed, the Spirit often gives us direction, reminding us of Scripture we have read before (John 14:26).

HOW SHOULD WE STUDY THE BIBLE?

There are many different ways to study the Bible. One good way is to take a particular subject, such as love or grace, and with the aid of a concordance or reference books, study what the Bible has to say on that subject. Another way is to study the lives of various individuals, such as David or Paul.

Perhaps the best Bible study method for beginners is to study a book at a time, so as to follow what the author is saying from start to finish. The important thing is to get started and to form a consistent habit of Bible study. Here are some principles you will find helpful for whatever method you choose:

- **Be consistent.** Daily Bible study is best, even if there are some days you only have time to read a few verses.
- **Don't rush.** It is best to read slowly, carefully and prayerfully, remaining alert to what God may be wanting to teach you in the passage.
- **Keep a record.** Write down special insights or lessons for future reference.
- **Commit to memory.** Memorize verses that have special meaning or importance, so they will become a part of your life.
- **Be systematic.** Develop a study plan that covers the whole Bible.
- **Be social.** Study both alone and with others, so you can have the benefit of others' insights while also learning to understand the Bible for yourself.
- **Believe.** Always come to the Bible in an attitude of faith and humility, trusting God to speak to you and maintaining an open heart to receive.
- **Be persistent.** Do not be surprised or discouraged when you come across something you don't understand. Your comprehension will increase as you study more and more. The rule is never to let something you don't understand obscure something that is clear.
- **Be obedient.** Always strive to put into practice what you read. The doers of the Word are those who really understand it and who experience its blessings (James 1:22).
- **Depend on the Holy Spirit.** We are blessed to have the author of Scripture, the Spirit of God Himself, present within us to help us understand it. Ask Him to give you insight into His Word.

Read the Bible! Give God's Word a central place in your life, and don't let anything crowd it out. Jesus taught, "Man shall not live on bread alone, but on every word that comes from the mouth of God (Matthew 4:4).

REFLECT & RESPOND

1. How would you explain to someone how the Bible came to be?

2. Who is the Bible about? Does this help you understand how the Old and New Testaments fit together into one book?

3. Why is the Bible such an important book?

Q&A

Read 2 Timothy 3:14-17.

1. What can Bible study do for us (v. 15)?

2. What is Scripture useful for?

3. What will happen if we study and obey the Bible (v. 17)?

Read Psalm 19:7-14.

4. How does the psalmist describe God's Word?

5. What things can it do for us?

6. Make a plan for regular Bible study, and start right away!

FOR FURTHER STUDY

Arnold, Clinton E. *How We Got the Bible: A Visual Journey.* Grand Rapids, MI: Zondervan, 2008.

Duvall, J. Scott and J. Daniel Hayes. *Journey Into God's Word: Your Guide to Understanding and Applying the Bible.* Grand Rapids, MI: Zondervan, 2008.

Sproul, R. C. *Can I Trust the Bible?* Orlando, FL: Reformation Trust, 2009.

CHAPTER FOUR:
God Comes

THE UNIQUENESS OF JESUS CHRIST

Of everyone who has walked the earth throughout all human history, Jesus Christ stands out as utterly unique.

His birth was unique.

Jesus is the only person ever born of a virgin. This is because He had no human father. He was conceived through the work of the Holy Spirit, and His father was God Himself (Luke 1:26-35).

His life was unique.

Jesus is the only person who never committed a single sin (1 Peter 2:22). He lived a life of perfect love and righteousness. Even His enemies could find no substantive charge to bring against Him (Mark 14:55).

His words were unique (John 7:46).

Though untrained and from a little-known family in a small town, Jesus debated and refuted the most highly regarded scholars of His day (Luke 20:26, 40). The people who heard Him speak recognized a unique wisdom and authority in His voice (Matthew 7:28, 29). Though He wrote nothing, Jesus' words have been recorded and reproduced in more languages and have sold more copies than any other book ever written. His words have stood the test of time, changing individual lives, influencing nations, and guiding whole civilizations for almost 2000 years.

His deeds were unique.

Jesus did things no man before or since has done (John 21:25). He performed miracles showing His power over disease (Matthew 4:23), over Satan and demons (Luke 11:14), over the forces of nature (Mark 4:39-41), and even over death itself (John 11:43, 44).

His death was unique.

Being perfectly righteous, Jesus was the only person whose death was wholly avoidable and undeserved. Though He didn't have to die, Jesus chose to suffer a shameful and torturous death on the cross, dying in our place (Philippians 2:6-8). His death wrought changes in the heavens (Matthew 27:45), on the earth (Matthew 27:51-53), and in the hearts of people (Matthew 27:54).

His resurrection was unique.

Jesus did not remain dead, but came forth out of the tomb on the third day. He alone conquered death, bursting its bonds and asserting His authority over it (Revelation 1:18). After forty days, He ascended bodily into heaven (Acts 1:9-11). He lives and reigns forevermore (1 Peter 3:22)!

His place in history is unique.

No individual ever had greater influence upon the course of history. No name has inspired more acts of heroism, mercy, and devotion. Jesus' birth marks the dividing line of history, for after His coming nothing has been the same.

WHO IS JESUS CHRIST?

Who is this man called Jesus, unique in so many ways?

Jesus Christ is God.

Christianity is the only religion whose founder not only claimed to show the way to God, but also actually claimed to *be* God. Indeed,

He is the only person who could make such a claim and be believed. Only His divinity serves to explain all about Him that is unique.

Before His birth in Bethlehem, Jesus, the Son of God, existed eternally with the Father in heaven (John 1:1, 2). His birth to Mary marked His entrance into the world as a human being, not the beginning of His life (John 8:58). His life had no beginning, for there was never a time when He did not exist. Before all worlds were created, before time itself, and from all eternity the Son of God was.

Not only did Christ exist before the worlds were made, but it was through Him that they were brought into being (John 1:3). Christ is the eternal Word of God through whom creation was spoken into existence. He is both Creator and sustainer of all things (Colossians 1:16, 17).

Jesus claimed a special relationship with God the Father, a unity that could only mean that He, too, was divine (John 10:30, 38). He claimed for Himself the authority to forgive sins (Mark 2:5-7), and He accepted worship that is due God alone (John 9:38). For these things, He was put to death as a blasphemer (John 19:7), and He refused to deny that He was more than a human being in order to save Himself (Luke 22:70).

Jesus' disciples came to recognize His divinity, and they offered Him their worship (Luke 24:52) and obedience. They gave their lives to make Him known throughout the world. Countless Christians since have believed their testimony and have come to know for themselves that Jesus Christ is God (John 20:31).

Jesus Christ is a human being.

The incarnation is perhaps the most incredible miracle imaginable. The eternal God actually became a human being and walked the earth He had spoken into existence (John 1:14). The Creator entered into His creation and became a part of it.

This was not a pretense or a charade. God did not just put on the disguise of a human being. He actually entered into and experienced real human life (Hebrews 2:17). He was born into the world a helpless infant, and He grew from childhood into adulthood. He laughed and cried, He worked and played, and He grew tired and rested. He felt the full range of emotions all human beings are subject to: sorrow and joy, fear and frustration, love and anger.

As a human being, Jesus experienced everything you and I experience in this life. Even though He never sinned, He still suffered the consequences of the sins of others. He knew disappointment, rejection, and betrayal. He faced every temptation that we face, and to an even greater degree, for He resisted unto the end (Hebrews 4:15).

As a real human being, Jesus died a real death. The cross He hung upon had real splinters. Real nails pierced His flesh and held Him there. Real blood spilled from His veins and dripped to the earth. Jesus lived and died as a real human being.

Through one person, sin came into the world, bringing death with it (Romans 5:12). Through another person, righteousness conquered sin, and life replaced death (Romans 5:16-18). Who was this person? The one who was God, the God who was a human being, the God-man Jesus Christ.

Jesus Christ is Savior.

The angel who appeared to Mary told her that she was to name her coming child "Jesus" (Luke 1:31). The name means "the Lord saves," for Jesus was to be the one through whom God would save humanity from the destruction of sin. Jesus was also given the title "Christ," meaning "anointed one." He was the one whose coming the old covenant prophets foretold, the one whom God anointed to bring about the salvation of His people.

This was the purpose of Jesus' coming into the world. This was the reason He was born, the reason He lived, the reason He died, and the reason He rose from the grave. It is the reason He carries on, even now, a ministry of intercession before the Father in heaven (Hebrews 7:25). He was given the task of saving sinful people separated from God, and He accomplished it completely (John 19:30). Through Jesus, the door is open for anyone to be saved from sin and to return to God. He is the Savior!

If we reject Jesus, we reject any hope of salvation, for there is no salvation apart from Him. He is the Savior, and there is no other (Acts 4:12). There is but one mediator, one link between human beings and God, and that is the God-man Jesus Christ (1 Timothy 2:5). There is but one way back to God for sinful people (John 14:6). We must come as God has determined or not at all.

Jesus Christ is Lord.

Some think of Jesus only as the meek and humble carpenter from Nazareth, who preached love for one's enemies and offered no resistance to those who arrested and executed Him. Jesus is truly the Lamb of God, who in submission to the will of God the Father, offered Himself as a sacrifice for our sin. But because of His obedience, Jesus has now been given the place of highest authority and the name that is above every name (Philippians 2:9). He is now the Lamb upon the throne, who rules over all (Revelation 5:6).

Jesus is called not only the Lamb, but also the Lion (Revelation 5:5). When He returns in power and glory, He will complete His triumph over His already vanquished enemies. At that time, all will bow and acknowledge Him as Lord (Philippians 2:10, 11). He will be the judge and ruler of all the nations (Revelation 19:15), and He will reign as King of kings forever (Revelation 11:15).

Though He is not yet universally recognized as King, even now Jesus has been given all authority in heaven and on earth (Matthew 28:18). All who now oppose Him do so in vain. He patiently endures their rebellion, while giving them time to repent and using their resistance for His own purposes (Romans 2:2-4). All must submit to His will, whether voluntarily or not.

Jesus is Lord of all the world and all of life. He is Lord not only of the Church, but also of every institution and individual. He reigns not only over the "religious" parts of our lives, but also over every part: our homes and our jobs, our time and our money, our family and our nation.

There is nothing that is not under Jesus' authority, nothing that is not to be submitted to His Lordship. We must strive to do His will in all things and work to see His will done in all areas of life, in all parts of the world. For Jesus is Lord of all!

"Worthy is the Lamb, who was slain, to receive power and wealth and wisdom and strength and honor and glory and praise!" (Revelation 5:12).

REFLECT & RESPOND

1. Do your best to recall the ways that Jesus is utterly unique.

2. Why is it important to believe that Jesus is fully God *and* fully human?

3. What does it mean that Jesus is your Savior and Lord?

Q&A
Read John 1:1-18.

1. Where was Jesus before the world was made?

2. What role did Jesus play in creation?

3. What does it mean to say, "the Word became flesh"?

4. What did Jesus come into the world to bring?

5. If no one has seen God, how can we know what He is like?

FOR FURTHER STUDY

Driscoll, Mark and Gary Breshears. *Vintage Jesus: Timely Answers to Timely Questions*. Wheaton, IL: Crossway Books, 2008.

Erickson, Millard J. *The Word Became Flesh: A Contemporary Incarnational Christology*. Grand Rapids, MI: Baker Academic, 1996.

Wright, N. T. *The Challenge of Jesus: Rediscovering Who Jesus Was and Is*. Downers Grove, IL: InterVarsity Press, 1999.

CHAPTER FIVE:
God Dwells

WHO IS THE HOLY SPIRIT?

The Holy Spirit is not some kind of vague, impersonal force or influence. He is a divine person who speaks (Acts 10:19), hears (John 16:13), and acts (John 16:14). He can be lied to (Acts 5:3), grieved (Ephesians 4:30), and blasphemed (Matthew 12:31). The Holy Spirit is not an emanation from God; He *is* God, in co-equal union with God the Father and God the Son.

This present age is preeminently the age of the Holy Spirit. As Jesus has now ascended to join the Father in heaven, the Holy Spirit is the member of the Trinity with whom we have the most direct contact. While God the Father is God *transcendent*, majestic and holy, better than His creation, the Holy Spirit is God *immanent*, present everywhere in the midst of creation. While Jesus is Emmanuel, God *with* us, the Holy Spirit is the Comforter, God *within* us.

WHAT DOES THE HOLY SPIRIT DO?

The Holy Spirit is the divine agent who carries out the Father's will in His dealings with believers. His activity begins even before conversion, when He convicts the sinner of guilt and draws him to Christ (John 16:8). Then it is the Holy Spirit who regenerates the repentant sinner, reviving the dead spirit within and giving new life

(John 3:5, 6). He then comes to live within the believer (Romans 8:9); His presence is a seal of ownership marking the Christian as God's property (2 Corinthians 1:22).

The Holy Spirit directs and empowers every step of the Christian life. Jesus said that the Holy Spirit would take His place, becoming to all believers everything that Jesus was to His twelve disciples (John 14:16). Jesus called Him another *Paraclete* (a Greek term translated Advocate, Comforter, or Helper), suggesting one who is with us at all times and upon whom we can depend completely.

The list of the Holy Spirit's activities is endless. He guides us into the truth, and He reveals to us the things of God and of Christ (John 16:13-15). He leads us to do God's will (Galatians 5:18). He speaks to us and through us (Acts 10:19; Mark 13:11). He fills our hearts with the love of God (Romans 5:5). He empowers us (Acts 1:8), inspires us (2 Peter 1:21), prays for us (Romans 8:26), and gives gifts to us (1 Corinthians 12:11). Our Teacher, our Guide, our Strength, our Companion—the Holy Spirit is all these things and more.

In all this, it is important to note that the Holy Spirit does not draw attention to Himself (John 16:13). The purpose of His ministry is to glorify and bear witness to Christ (John 16:14). He inspired the Bible whose theme is Christ, He convicts sinners to turn to Christ the Savior, He works to form the image of Christ in believers, and He joins believers together into the body of Christ, the Church. Just as Jesus sought throughout His ministry to glorify His Father (John 17:4), the Holy Spirit now seeks to glorify Christ. Everything He does is meant to exalt Jesus. Where the Holy Spirit works, Jesus is glorified.

WHAT IS THE BAPTISM IN THE HOLY SPIRIT?

Before Jesus ascended into heaven after His resurrection, He told His disciples to wait in Jerusalem to receive the gift His Father promised (Acts 1:4, 5). On the day of Pentecost, about ten days after Jesus' ascension, some 120 believers were gathered for prayer when they received the promised gift: the baptism in the Holy Spirit (Acts 2:1-4). Peter preached to the crowd that had gathered to see what was happening, and he made it clear to them that the promise was not limited to a certain group or a certain time; it was for all who would put their faith in Christ (Acts 2:38, 39). The baptism in the Holy Spirit is for us today as well.

Baptism in the Spirit is compared to baptism in water (Acts 1:5), suggesting the image of being immersed or engulfed. The Holy Spirit dwells within every Christian, but baptism means being filled with the Spirit in an abundant measure, even to overflowing. As we yield ourselves totally, the Holy Spirit fills us completely.

Prophets and priests in the Old Testament were anointed with oil, a symbol of the Holy Spirit, as a sign of being chosen and set apart to serve God. The New Testament teaches that all believers are priests set apart for God (1 Peter 2:9), gifted to serve Him (1 Corinthians 12:7). The power to serve God is through the baptism in the Holy Spirit (Acts 1:8).

WHAT SIGNS ACCOMPANY THE BAPTISM IN THE HOLY SPIRIT?

When the 120 believers received the baptism in the Holy Spirit on the day of Pentecost, several unusual signs or manifestations accompanied the experience: a sound like rushing wind, what seemed to be tongues of fire, and utterances of praise to God in languages unknown to the speakers (Acts 2:1-4). Similar remarkable things happened on other occasions when people received this baptism in the Spirit (Acts 8:14-17; 10:44-47; 19:1-6).

Different people react to the Spirit's infilling in different ways. Some laugh, while others weep. Some shout and dance, while others are more restrained. The common initial evidence, however, is "speaking in tongues": the Holy Spirit gives words to speak in a language we do not know, so that we praise God without understanding what we are saying.

Of course, the most important sign of the Spirit's infilling is what follows: a life yielded to God, directed, and empowered for effective witnessing (Acts 1:8).

HOW DO WE RECEIVE THE BAPTISM IN THE HOLY SPIRIT?

Like everything else in the Christian life, the baptism in the Holy Spirit comes by grace through faith. We must believe that God has promised the gift to us (Acts 2:39), and then receive it.

The basis of the outpouring of the Holy Spirit is the exaltation of Christ (Acts 2:33). Because Christ died and rose again, we can be saved and sanctified. Because Christ has been exalted to the right hand of God, we can receive the baptism in the Holy Spirit. The experience comes to us as a gift, not because we do anything to earn or deserve it, but because it is the sign of Christ's ascension to reign.

Believing in Christ's exaltation and the Father's promise, we have only to ask Christ to baptize us. Sometimes He pours out this blessing even before we ask (Acts 10:44, 45). Sometimes the gift is given through the laying on of hands (Acts 8:17). But we are encouraged to ask in faith, assured of God's desire to give us this gift (Luke 11:13).

The Holy Spirit invariably comes in an atmosphere of praise (Acts 2:11; 10:46). This is only natural, for it is the Spirit's ministry to exalt Christ. Therefore, we are most likely to receive the baptism when we are praising God with our hearts and mouths. We should focus our attention on Christ, not on our surroundings, our feelings, or the words we are speaking. Remember, too, that speaking in tongues is a cooperative effort: the Spirit gives us the words, but we must open our mouths and speak.

WHAT IF WE DON'T RECEIVE THE BAPTISM RIGHT AWAY?

We must be willing to persevere in seeking this gift (Luke 11:8-10). We must not become discouraged if there is some delay in receiving the baptism in the Holy Spirit. If there is some hindrance in our life, our faith, or our understanding, God will reveal it to us. He is faithful, and He will reward those who seek Him and His gifts (Hebrews 11:6).

WHAT ARE THE GIFTS OF THE SPIRIT?

The Holy Spirit gives various gifts to believers to be used to encourage and build up the church (1 Corinthians 12:7). The gifts the Spirit gives may be divided into manifestation and ministry gifts.

Manifestation gifts are given to an individual for use on a particular occasion, and they are not the permanent possession of the individual. The Holy Spirit uses the individual as a channel through which the gift operates at that time. Manifestation gifts include the following, but we should not assume that the list is exhaustive (1 Corinthians 12:7-10):

1. A **word of wisdom** enabling us to solve a problem or handle a difficult situation we are faced with (see Acts 15:13-29).
2. A **word of knowledge** imparting information beyond our natural means of knowing (see Acts 5:1-5).
3. Extraordinary **faith** to believe God for the impossible (see Acts 27:21-25).
4. Gifts of **healing** to effect miraculous cures of various diseases (see Acts 3:1-8).
5. **Prophecy**, a word of exhortation or encouragement from God to His people (see Acts 11:27-30).
6. **Miraculous powers** of various kinds (see Acts 5:12).
7. **Discernment** to detect the spiritual source of someone's words or deeds (see Acts 13:6-12).
8. **Speaking in tongues**, the supernatural ability to pray to or praise God in a language unknown to the speaker (see Acts 2:4-11).
9. **Interpretation of tongues**, the supernatural ability to interpret a tongue so that others can understand and be edified (see Acts 10:44-47).

In addition to the manifestation gifts, the Spirit also gives *ministry gifts*. These gifts are given to an individual on a long-term basis to be exercised regularly in his or her ministry. Every Christian is gifted to contribute to the functioning of the church body. Body ministry gifts comprise all the multifaceted gifts distributed to the believers to do the work of the church (Romans 12:6-8). Equipping ministry gifts are given and used especially for training believers to carry on the ministry (Ephesians 4:11-16).

HOW ARE SPIRITUAL GIFTS TO BE EXERCISED?

There are four principles to guide us in the exercise of the gifts of the Spirit:

1. The gifts are given for the building up of the church, not for the exaltation of any individual (1 Corinthians 12:7).
2. God graciously gives gifts to individuals, and so they are not a sign of holiness or spiritual maturity (compare 1 Corinthians 1:7 and 3:1).
3. The exercise of the gifts is under the control of the individual, who is responsible to use them in obedience to the will of God (1 Corinthians 14:31-33). We are not without error, and we can misuse God's gifts, so our exercise of them is subject to the judgment of those in authority (1 Corinthians 14:29).
4. The gifts are always to be exercised in love (1 Corinthians 13:1, 2).

WHAT ARE THE FRUIT OF THE SPIRIT?

Perhaps the most important ministry of the Holy Spirit is the development of Christ's character in His people. The fruit that comes forth in our attitudes and actions most clearly reveals the Holy Spirit's presence in our lives. Love, joy, peace, patience, kindness, goodness, faithfulness, gentleness, and self-control—these are the fruit of the Spirit's activity in our hearts (Galatians 5:22, 23). Unlike the gifts of the Spirit, which vary from believer to believer, every Christian should exhibit all of these qualities. May the Lord fill us with His Spirit, in order that Christ may be formed and exalted in us!

REFLECT & RESPOND

1. Do your best to recall the person and work of the Holy Spirit.

2. What gifts of the Spirit have you experienced so far?

3. Why is the Holy Spirit able to develop Christlike character in a Christian?

Q&A

Read John 14:15-27.

1. What names does Jesus give to the Holy Spirit?

2. What does Jesus say the Holy Spirit will do?

3. Why do you think the Holy Spirit is called the "Spirit of Christ"?

Read Ephesians 4:29–5:2.

4. What do you think it means to "grieve the Holy Spirit"? (4:30)

Read 1 Thessalonians 5:19-22.

5. What do you think it means to "quench the Spirit"? (5:19)

FOR FURTHER STUDY

Chan, Francis. *Forgotten God: Reversing Our Tragic Neglect of the Holy Spirit*. Colorado Springs, CO: David C. Cook, 2009.

Fee, Gordon D. *Paul, the Spirit, and the People of God*. Peabody, MA: Hendrickson, 1996.

Grudem, Wayne. ed. *Are Miraculous Gifts for Today?* Grand Rapids, MI: Zondervan, 1996.

CHAPTER SIX:
God Transforms

When we put our faith in Christ, God forgives us of our sins and makes us a part of His family. But this is only the beginning of what God wants to do in our lives. Becoming a Christian is only the first step in our walk with God, and many glorious things await us on the path ahead.

God's marvelous plan for our lives encompasses our past, present, and future (Romans 8:29, 30):

1. **Justification** is deliverance from the penalty of sin. Through Christ's death on the cross, the sins of our past are forgiven and we are justified (declared righteous) in God's sight.
2. **Sanctification** is deliverance from the power of sin. Right now, God is at work sanctifying us, making us more and more like Christ.
3. **Glorification** is deliverance from the presence of sin. At Christ's future return, we will be transformed into an immortal state in which we share in the glory of Christ.

It is important for us to realize what God's purpose is for us, in order that we may cooperate with Him and not hinder what He is trying to accomplish in our lives. God's goal is to conform us to the image of Christ, and everything that He brings into our lives or brings us through has this end in mind. This is no mere suggestion; the will of God is that believers be sanctified (1 Thessalonians 4:3).

Understanding what God has in mind for us, we must give ourselves fully to the accomplishing of this purpose. It is not enough simply to sit back and wait for God to do it all; we must focus our desires and devote our energies toward reaching the goal God has set for us (Philippians 3:12-14).

WHY DO WE NEED TO BE SANCTIFIED?

After we become Christians, shall we go on living just as before? Since God has forgiven our sins, shall we just keep on sinning (Romans 6:1)? Of course not! God has better things in mind for us than that. God's goal for His people is nothing less than holiness (Hebrews 12:14). God wants us to live lives that reflect His righteousness and glorify Him (Matthew 5:48).

However, there is a problem that hinders this purpose of God for us. In fact, *we* are the problem! The sins we committed have been forgiven, but the sinner who committed them remains. The source of our sin problem lies within our own hearts (Matthew 15:18, 19).

When we are born again, the Spirit of God gives us new life. But the old habits, attitudes, and thought patterns remain. And so a conflict arises between the old life and the new (Galatians 5:17). There is a struggle within us, as both the old nature and the new nature strive for mastery in our lives.

WHAT CAN BE DONE ABOUT THE PROBLEM OF OUR SIN NATURE?

God did not intend for us to be mired in a continual state of conflict over the issue of sin. He did not intend for us to live defeated lives, but to have victory over sin. In fact, God dealt with our need for sanctification at the same time and in the same way as He dealt with our need for forgiveness: through the death of Christ on the cross.

When Christ was crucified, He died in our place. This means not only that He died as our *substitute*, taking upon Himself the penalty due our sins, but also that He died as our *representative*, undergoing death on our behalf. His death is *our* death.

God has passed the sentence upon us as sinners: the sentence of death (Romans 6:23). That sentence was carried out when Christ was crucified. When we put our faith in Christ, we are united with Him; thus, His death on the cross becomes our death as well (Romans 6:3). The sinner that you used to be, the sinner that is the source of all the problems with sin in your life, has been put to death on the cross of Christ.

God's method of dealing with our sinful selves is not to strengthen us so as to enable us to resist sin, but rather to put us to death so that sin will no longer have us in its power (Romans 6:6, 7). Our deliverance from sin comes in the form of death. In Christ we die unto sin, in order that we may live for God (Romans 6:8-11).

HOW CAN WE EXPERIENCE DELIVERANCE FROM SIN?

On our own we can't; we're powerless to do so. However, through the indwelling Holy Spirit, God enables us to live more and more like Jesus. God enables our growth in Christlikeness (Philippians 2:12, 13). In addition, we obtain deliverance from sin's power in just the same way we obtain forgiveness: through faith in Christ. We believe that Christ's death paid the penalty for our sins, and so we are forgiven. We believe that in Christ our sinful nature was put to death, and so we are dead to sin. In both cases, we appropriate what Christ has done and count on it to be true, not just for humanity in general, but for us personally (Romans 6:11). As salvation is a work of God's grace, so also this death to sin is a work of God's grace.

Here is where the problem comes in: most of us don't want to die. Before we can receive forgiveness in Christ, we must be willing to confess our sins. In the same way, before we can be delivered from sin's power, we must be willing to assent to the death of our old, sinful selves. We must die so that Christ may live in us.

What does it mean to give ourselves up unto death? It means not holding on to any sin, but letting go and allowing every unholy desire in us to die. It means no longer running our own lives, but taking ourselves out of the way in order to make room for Christ to reign.

We cannot hope to find deliverance from sin's power as long as we insist on maintaining control of our own lives. If we try to be our own master, we will only end up as slaves to sin (John 8:34). We can find freedom from sin only in offering ourselves as slaves unto God (Romans 6:16).

One meaning of the New Testament word for sanctify is "to set apart." If we consecrate our bodies to God and set them apart for His use, they will no longer be available for sin's use (Romans 6:13).

Sanctification has both a negative and a positive aspect. It means saying "no" to sin and "yes" to God. Both of these are essential. We cannot serve God unless we have given up sin. We cannot be free from sin unless we allow God to become our new master (Colossians 3:9, 10). But if we are willing, Christ's death to sin becomes ours, and His life for God becomes ours as well (Romans 6:8-10).

DOES SANCTIFICATION MEAN WE NO LONGER SIN?

Sanctification is not sinless perfection. We never reach the place in this life where we cannot sin. We never get beyond the reach of temptation, but we must always be vigilant so that we do not fall into sin. We can always choose to submit to sin's power; we can still say "yes" to it.

On the other hand, it is not true that as long as we are in this life we *must* sin. God has provided for us a means of deliverance through Christ's death for us and His life in us. We can live in victory over sin; we can say "no" to it.

IS SANCTIFICATION A ONCE-FOR-ALL EXPERIENCE OR A LIFETIME PROCESS?

It is a combination of both. We enter into the experience of sanctification through a crisis decision of consecration, but the process continues throughout our lives as God works to conform us to the image of Christ.

Broadly speaking, we can identify four stages of God's sanctifying work in our lives:

1. **The new birth**, when our sins are forgiven and we are washed clean from the stain of sin (Titus 3:5).

2. A **crisis experience** of sanctification when we count ourselves dead to sin, its power over us is broken, and our hearts are purified (Romans 6:11; Acts 15:9; James 4:8). Some believe this coincides with the new birth.

3. **Continual spiritual growth**, as day-by-day we mature and become more and more like Christ (John 17:17; Hebrews 6:1).

4. **Glorification**, when we see Christ face to face and are finally perfected, in a state of being where we will never sin again (1 John 3:2).

WHAT HAPPENS IF WE SIN?

If we do sin, it is not the end. We have not lost our salvation. Christ continues to pray for us, for our forgiveness and restoration (1 John 2:1). But sin breaks our fellowship with God, and it puts us in danger of leaving the path and wandering away from God for good. Therefore, sin should be confessed immediately, so that we can receive God's forgiveness and our relationship with Him can be restored right away. We must not allow our sin to drive us away from God out of shame or fear. Rather, sin should drive us to Him for forgiveness and cleansing (1 John 1:9).

Sin is serious business. It must never be taken lightly, for it is deadly, it can destroy the soul, and it is offensive to God. But we need not despair, for God's grace is greater than our sin (Romans 5:20, 21). If we turn to Him in repentance and faith, He will restore us.

WHAT IS THE SANCTIFIED LIFE LIKE?

The sanctified life is not stuffy, solemn, and holier-than-thou. We are not talking about a legalism that judges oneself and others on the basis of mere outward dos and don'ts (Colossians 2:20-23). The focus is on the inner condition of the heart, where true holiness shines forth in joyful freedom and love for others (Galatians 5:13, 14).

The sanctified life is a Christ-like life, where the positive qualities of Christ's character are seen in us (Galatians 5:22-24). Indeed, the sanctified life is Christ's life in us, as Paul explains in Galatians 2:20: "I have been crucified with Christ. It is no longer I who live, but

Christ who lives in me. And the life I now live in the flesh I live by faith in the Son of God, who loved me and gave himself for me."

The sanctified life is an exchanged life: I trade my sinful life for Christ's righteous one. I die in Him; He lives in me. Thank God that He has provided a way out of sin's dreadful bondage through Jesus Christ our Lord (Romans 7:25)!

REFLECT & RESPOND

1. How would you explain the place of sanctification in the Christian life?

2. Why do you need to be sanctified? How can you be sanctified?

3. How do you know if your life looks more and more like Christ's?

Q&A

Read John 15:1-11.

1. Who is the vine? Who are the branches? Who is the gardener?

2. What can we do on our own, apart from Christ?

3. What does the Father do to make us more fruitful?

4. What does it mean to "remain in Christ"?

FOR FURTHER STUDY

Bridges, Jerry. *The Pursuit of Holiness*. Colorado Springs, CO: NavPress, 2006.

Mahaney, C. J. *Humility: True Greatness*. Colorado Springs, CO: Multnomah, 2005.

Whitney, Donald S. *Spiritual Disciplines for the Christian Life*. Colorado Springs, CO: NavPress, 1997.

CHAPTER SEVEN:
God Listens

WHAT IS PRAYER?

No human activity is more sublime, none more mysterious, than prayer. Through prayer, we actually speak to God, who created and sustains the universe.

And yet, at the same time, prayer is very simple. It involves only talking and listening, ordinary things we do every day. Prayer is merely conversing with God.

The Lord is a God who speaks. He is not a silent deity; it is His nature to communicate. And God has made us in such a way that we share this ability to communicate. He has given us mouths to speak and ears to hear, as well as the remarkable capacity to express ourselves through the medium of language.

Certainly God knows our innermost thoughts and feelings even without our putting them into words. Nevertheless, God desires the kind of communal relationship that comes only with our active participation. God wants us to talk with Him. He actually listens to what we have to say!

But prayer is not just talking to God. Prayer involves listening as well. Although He usually doesn't speak in an audible voice, God does often speak directly from His Spirit to ours. God's voice may come to us in the form of thoughts implanted in our minds, a leading toward a particular course of action, or new light, which enables us to see things in His Word with greater clarity.

But hearing from God requires concentration on our part, a conscious turning of our heart and attention toward Him. We must not monopolize our conversations with God, so filling our prayers with our own thoughts and desires that we fail to hear what He may be saying to us.

We must *want* to hear from God, and we must make room for Him to speak. If we do listen, we can be confident that God will speak, for it is His desire that we hear Him. And that is what makes prayer possible.

ARE THERE DIFFERENT KINDS OF PRAYER?

There are several different kinds of prayer, including:

Petition

We often think of prayer as asking God for something. This is called *petition*, and although it is not the only kind of prayer, it is an important one. God encourages us to bring all our needs to Him, including the basic necessities of life (Matthew 6:11).

The Bible is full of people who received what they asked for from God. Jesus told us plainly to "ask and you will receive, and your joy will be complete" (John 16:24). God takes pleasure in giving to His children. Of course, God sometimes has good reason to refuse the requests of His children. He knows what is best for us, and He also takes note of the motives behind our requests (James 4:3). But we should never hesitate to bring our needs and wants to our Father, for it is His delight to give.

Praise

Petition should be balanced with *praise*. Praise is glorifying God, telling Him of our love for Him. Rather than asking for something, we express our appreciation for all He has done for us. In the act of exalting God, our own souls are lifted up as well. God's people are a people of praise.

Confession

Honest and effective prayer includes *confession*. This means allowing the Spirit of God to convict us of our sins and responding in repentance and contrition. This requires humbling ourselves before God and being willing to face up to what we have done wrong. Sin will wreck our relationship with God, but "If we confess our sins, he is faithful and just and will forgive us our sins and purify us from all unrighteousness" (1 John 1:9).

Intercession

Intercession means praying to God on behalf of someone else. In this type of prayer, our focus is not on our own needs, but on those of others. Intercession gives us an amazing opportunity to help and influence others, as God moves in their lives in answer to our prayers. Indeed, praying for others is a great way to demonstrate our love for others. And God is pleased with us when we are unselfish enough to pray for someone else.

Communion

Finally, there is what we might call *communion*, when we simply open our hearts to God and share with Him our deepest feelings, thoughts, and dreams. Such intimate times of fellowship develop and enrich our relationship with God and draw us closer to Him.

HOW SHOULD WE PRAY?

There is no need to use formal or flowery language when we talk with God. He is more interested in the sincerity of our heart than in the eloquence of our speech. If we have trouble getting started, or if we find it difficult to put our thoughts into words, it can be helpful to use the prayers in Scripture as models. That is the purpose of what is known as the Lord's Prayer (Matthew 6:5-13).

There is no set pattern or posture which we must follow in prayer. We have the freedom to pray silently or aloud, with eyes open or closed, kneeling, standing, sitting, or lying down. We can pray in our native tongue and in a Holy Spirit-given prayer language. The important thing is to pray with reverence and sincerity.

WHEN SHOULD WE PRAY?

A Christian's prayer life should include all of the following:

1. **We should pray daily.** A specific time should be set aside for prayer each day, perhaps 10 to 15 minutes to start and more as we

become more comfortable and more proficient. Many Christians follow the pattern of Jesus in praying first thing in the morning, so as to draw close to God at the beginning of the day. Some make a practice of pausing at set times throughout the day for prayer (see Daniel 6:10). But whether you pray morning, afternoon, or evening, choose a time that fits your schedule and stick with it. Of course, interruptions will come and adjustments will sometimes have to be made. Don't be discouraged. The important thing is to develop a habit of daily prayer.

2. **We should pray with other Christians.** Our prayers gain strength when united with the prayers of others. We should participate in regular prayer meetings and join with others periodically to pray for revival or other special needs.

3. **We should pray on the spot.** Sometimes a given situation will call for immediate prayer. This includes everything from prayer for the sick or some other emergency to thanksgiving for a meal or a beautiful sunset. We should be ready to pray anytime, anywhere.

4. **We should pray continually.** Paul advises us to "pray continually" (1 Thessalonians 5:17). This involves learning to maintain a continual awareness of God's presence, a heart that seeks Him, and an ear open to His voice.

WHY SHOULD WE PRAY?

1. **God commands us to pray** (Isaiah 55:6; Matthew 6:9; Luke 18:1; 1 Thessalonians 5:17; etc.). This is reason enough!

2. **Prayer is necessary for our spiritual growth.** Prayer enriches our knowledge of God and deepens our relationship with Him, and it is a source of power for witnessing and holy living (John 15:7, 8).

3. **The Bible tells us we are blessed and God is blessed when we pray** (John 15:7). For one thing, God answers prayer (Jeremiah 33:3; Matthew 7:7-11; John 15:7). Our joy is made complete when we pray in line with God's Word (John 16:24). God is also blessed. He is glorified when we pray, as Jesus stated:

"And I will do whatever you ask in my name, so that the Father may be *glorified* in the Son" (John 14:13, emphasis added).

4. **God loves us and wants to spend time with us.** Our love for Him should cause us to seek out and spend time with Him. What a privilege to converse with the Creator of the universe, in whose mind is all knowledge and in whose hand is all power!

HOW CAN WE PRAY EFFECTIVELY?

First, simply pray. The more we pray, the more we will learn about prayer. It is also beneficial to study the prayers recorded in Scripture, to see how Christ, the apostles, and the prophets prayed. The Psalms can be especially helpful, for they express the wide range of emotions, desires, and concerns of the human heart. Listen to the prayers of mature believers. They have spent years cultivating an active prayer life. Above all, the Holy Spirit is there to help us to pray—and to pray for us and through us (Romans 8:26, 27).

Below is a brief list of things than can help or hinder our prayers:

Helps to Prayer

1. **Faith** (Matthew 21:21, 22). Our prayers are more effective when we see God for who He is and become confident in our Father's love and power. Our faith increases, not when we try to make ourselves believe, but when we meditate on God, His deeds, and His promises.

2. **Sincerity** (Hebrews 4:13). It is essential that we come to God in total openness and honesty. It is foolish to try to hide or disguise ourselves, and doing so only prevents Him from meeting our real needs.

3. **Righteousness** (James 5:16). We cannot live our lives any way we please, neglecting God and His Word, and then expect Him to respond when we want something from Him.

4. **Humility** (Psalm 131:1, 2). God hears those who realize their need for Him, not those who imagine themselves to be self-sufficient.

5. **Persistence** (Luke 11:5-10). Don't give up! The promise is there for those who persevere. God sometimes says *no*, but we shouldn't give up until He does.

Hindrances to Prayer

1. **Unbelief** (Matthew 13:58). Unbelief causes us to continue worrying and keeps us from leaving the problem with God. It can prevent us from being receptive to the answer or even seeing it when it comes.

2. **Hypocrisy** (Matthew 6:5-8). Prayer that seeks to appear "spiritual" will accomplish nothing beyond that.

3. **Pride** (Luke 18:9-14). Prayer that is focused on the self is not putting us in a position to receive anything from God.

4. **Sin** (Psalm 66:18). Unconfessed sin or an unrepentant heart will build a barrier that blocks the path of prayer.

5. **Selfishness** (James 4:3). God sees the motives behind our prayers. He is concerned not only with what we ask for, but also with why we ask.

6. **Broken Relationships** (1 Peter 3:7). The way we treat others can have a significant effect on the way God responds to us.

It is impossible to overestimate the importance of prayer. Let Jesus be our example: If He needed to spend much time in prayer, how much more so do we? Nothing can be accomplished without prayer, but with prayer, anything is possible!

REFLECT & RESPOND

1. What is the essence of biblical prayer?

2. How can you pray effectively?

3. Why do you think it's necessary for a Christian to pray?

Q&A

Read David's prayer in 1 Chronicles 17:16-27.

1. How would you describe David's attitude as he comes before God to pray?

2. What does David say about God in his prayer?

3. What does David thank God for?

4. What does David ask God for?

5. What motives can you see in David's prayer?

FOR FURTHER STUDY

Carson, D. A. *A Call to Spiritual Reformation: Priorities From Paul and His Prayers*. Grand Rapids, MI: Baker, 1992.

Miller, Paul E. *A Praying Life: Connecting With God in a Distracting World*. Colorado Springs, CO: NavPress, 2009.

Murray, Andrew. *With Christ in the School of Prayer*. Reprint. Peabody, MA: Hendrickson, 2007.

CHAPTER EIGHT:
God Gathers

WHAT IS THE CHURCH?

The Church is God's family.

In the New Testament, the word "church" is used to refer to those whom God has called out from the world to become His children. Whenever anyone puts their faith in Christ for salvation, they become a member of the family of God. The Church is made up of all of God's children all over the world—in every nation, of every ethnicity, and of all languages (Revelation 7:9).

As children of God our Father, all Christians are brothers and sisters. Our faith in Christ unites us, and the same Holy Spirit dwells within each of us (Ephesians 4:4-6). As members of the same family, it is natural for Christians to love one another, and this love proves we belong to Christ (John 13:35).

The Church is God's Temple.

In the past, God chose to dwell among His people, Israel, in a Temple made with human hands (2 Chronicles 7:1-3). But now He desires to dwell among His people, Christians, in a temple He is building Himself. The Church is God's temple, a house not made with human hands, a place where God Himself is pleased to dwell (Ephesians 2:19-22).

We sometimes refer to the building in which we worship as "the church," but this is not really correct. The Church is made of people, not bricks and mortar. We are all "living stones" (1 Peter 2:5), being built together to form God's house, with Jesus Christ as the cornerstone. What a glorious calling, to be a part of the temple where God lives!

The Church is the body of Christ.

When the Son of God became a human being, He walked the earth in a physical body just like yours and mine. When He ascended into heaven after His resurrection, He sent the Holy Spirit (also called the "Spirit of Christ") so that His presence would remain here on the earth. But He also maintains a physical presence here, a body for His Spirit to live in. The Church is now Christ's body on the earth (1 Corinthians 12:12, 13).

Just as our physical bodies are made up of many different parts with many different functions, so also Christ's body on earth is composed of many different people with many different roles and abilities (1 Corinthians 12:14-20). As members of the Church, we have different jobs according to the place God assigns us in the Body, but we all work together. Each member has its place; all are needed, and none are left out. It is only together that we can fulfill our role as the body of Christ, carrying out His will on the earth.

The Church is the bride of Christ.

When Jesus lived and ministered on earth, He never took a wife. But He shed His blood and sacrificed His life in order to cleanse and sanctify a people who would become His bride (Ephesians 5:25-27). The Church is called the bride of Christ because He loves us, and he wants to be united with us in an intimate relationship that will bear fruit for Him.

As Christ's bride, the Church is called to be pure and holy. We are to remain faithful to Him, never allowing the things of this world to steal our affections. As Christ has loved us supremely and sacrificially, so we give Him our love in return, and we faithfully await the day when He returns to take us to Himself (Revelation 19:7).

WHAT ABOUT ALL THE DIFFERENT CHURCHES?

There is a single global Church, a divinely created spiritual organism, which includes every genuine believer in Christ throughout the world. The members of God's Church are recorded in the Lamb's Book of Life, whether or not their names are found on the membership roll of any local body of believers. The unity of the Church is spiritual, not organizational.

The one universal Church of God is made up of many local churches, smaller expressions of the universal Church. In addition, these local churches often form larger groups or denominations in order to help each other and cooperate in serving God. Such denominations can combine the efforts of local churches to make them more effective. Denominations can also provide accountability and oversight to insure that local churches and pastors remain biblical in doctrine (what the church teaches) and practice (what the church does).

Some denominations came into being in order to preserve certain truths that were neglected at the time. Others were started in times of revival, when God was doing something that not all current churches were willing to accept. Today, different denominations typically reflect differences in styles of worship or disagreements over certain doctrines.

Denominations can play an important role in unifying and supervising local churches, and they are deserving of respect and loyalty for the work they do. But it is never God's will that they become sources of division among His people, competing with or attacking one another. God is pleased and glorified when Christians work and fellowship together across denominational lines, thus bearing witness to their unity in Christ.

WHAT IS THE STRUCTURE OF THE CHURCH?

There is only one head of the Church, Jesus Christ (Ephesians 1:22). He is the one supreme authority to which all believers must submit.

God has ordained that there be other leaders in the church to exercise authority in submission to Jesus. He has not given a detailed blueprint as to how churches should be organized, which leaves congregations and denominations with a great deal of freedom to establish their own structure within the guidelines of Scripture.

According to Scripture, the spiritual leaders in the local church are elders. Sometimes called pastors (shepherds), bishops, or overseers, these leaders are responsible for the spiritual oversight of the flock (the people in a local church) under their care. They are to insure that the members of the church are taught the truth and built up in the faith, and they are responsible for exercising discipline when necessary. They are to be obeyed (Hebrews 13:17) and honored (1 Timothy 5:17). They must meet certain standards of character and conduct (1 Timothy 3:1-7).

Deacons have responsibility for the business affairs of the church and the physical needs of its members (Acts 6:1-4). They, too, must meet standards of dependability and trustworthiness (1 Timothy 3:8-13).

Some Christians may function in the roles of apostle, prophet, or evangelist (Ephesians 4:11). These are not local church offices. These individuals are called and gifted to serve a broader scope, often outside of (but still accountable to) a local church.

The church is free to select and appoint other officers and leaders as necessary. But all leadership in God's church is to be servant leadership (1 Peter 5:1-3). While God gives authority to those who watch over His people, it is an authority always to be exercised in love, following Christ's example (John 13:13-17).

WHAT DOES THE CHURCH DO?

The church ministers to God.

The church is called to *worship*. We were redeemed in order to praise and glorify our God (1 Peter 2:9). God's people are a people of praise, for they have tasted the goodness of the Lord and know His marvelous love and grace.

As a church, we gather to unite our voices in songs of praise and testify to what the Lord has done for us. We lift our hands and our hearts up to the Lord, offering ourselves individually and corporately as living sacrifices unto Him (Romans 12:1). God is worthy of our worship, and it is our privilege and our delight to give our best to honor and praise Him.

The church ministers to its members.

The church is called to *discipleship*. The members of the body are to use their gifts to serve and build up one another, so that the whole body will grow into what it is meant to be in Christ (Ephesians 4:11-13). This growth takes place through several kinds of ministry (Acts 2:42):

1. **Prayer.** The church comes together to pray, the members interceding for one another's needs and finding strength in united prayer.
2. **Preaching.** The church gathers to hear the Word of God proclaimed and explained, the members receiving its truth to penetrate and transform their minds and hearts.
3. **Fellowship.** The church partakes together of the Lord's Supper; the members proclaim their unity in Christ, encourage each other, bear each other's burdens, share with those in need, and simply love each other.

The church ministers to the world.

The church is called to *witness*. It is the responsibility of the church to proclaim the message of Christ, both in the local community and to the world at large (Acts 1:8). We must share the gospel where we live and also send missionaries to other lands (Matthew 28:19, 20).

We bear witness to Christ through word and deed, both explaining and demonstrating the truth of the gospel. The love and unity we demonstrate as Christians serve as a powerful testimony to the reality of Christ among us (John 17:23).

Above all, we are called as a church to follow in the footsteps of Christ, for we are His body on the earth (John 17:18). We are to pattern our ministry after His, speaking His words, doing His works, and loving with His love through His Spirit who lives within us (John 14:12).

IS IT NECESSARY TO JOIN A LOCAL CHURCH?

There are two powerful reasons every Christian should belong to a local church.

1. You need the local church. As believers in Christ, we all belong to His worldwide Church, but we can only experience what this means as part of a local fellowship of believers. The local church provides nurturing for our growth, encouragement when we are struggling, instruction in the truth, and protection from the enemy. As brothers and sisters in Christ, we pray together, laugh together, cry together, and live together (1 Corinthians 12:26).

We are all members of the body of Christ, but no member can function on its own. Separated from the rest of the body, it is dead and useless. You can never achieve God's purpose for your life alone, for you were made to fit into your place in the body. God has gifted all of us to work for Him, but none of us is gifted to work alone.

2. The local church needs you. The local church needs your ministry. The church is not complete without you. The gifts God has given you are meant to be used to help your fellow Christians (1 Corinthians 14:26). You may think there is nothing you can do, but God knows better. He has no useless members in His body (1 Corinthians 12:27).

The local church needs your prayers. The church leadership and the rest of your fellow believers need your prayer support. You need to pray for them and with them.

The local church needs your financial support. The tasks God has called His church to do require the resources of His people. If the local church is to fulfill its calling to worship the Lord, disciple believers, and share the gospel at home and abroad, you must contribute.

The Lord urges us to commit ourselves to the local church (Hebrews 10:24, 25). Faithfulness to His body is faithfulness to Him.

REFLECT & RESPOND

1. What is the relationship (differences and similarities) between the universal Church and a local church?

2. What is the church called to do?

3. Do you think you need to be a part of a local church? Why or why not?

Q&A
Read Ephesians 4:1-16.

1. What are some different aspects of the unity of the church (vv. 4-6)?

2. What must we do to maintain this unity (vv. 1-3)?

3. For what purpose does Christ give different ministers to the church (vv. 11-13)?

4. What happens when the church functions as it should (vv. 14-16)?

FOR FURTHER STUDY

Dever, Mark. *Nine Marks of a Healthy Church*. Wheaton, IL: Crossway Books, 2004.

DeYoung, Kevin and Ted Kluck. *Why We Love the Church: In Praise of Institutions and Organized Religion*. Chicago, IL: Moody, 2009.

Jones, Timothy Paul. *Christian History Made Easy: 13 Weeks to a Better Understanding of Church History*. Torrance, CA: Rose, 2009.

CHAPTER NINE:
God Reminds

An *ordinance* is an outward sign of a spiritual reality. Jesus instituted two ordinances (so called because Christ ordained them) that the church has practiced ever since its inception: baptism in water and the Lord's Supper, also known as Communion. Some church traditions call these *sacraments*, which are an outward and visible sign of an inward and spiritual grace. These ordinances have an important place in the life of every believer.

WHAT IS WATER BAPTISM?

Water baptism is typically the first act of obedience in the life of a new Christian. Unlike Communion, which is repeated again and again, baptism is a onetime ceremony that needs never to be repeated. It symbolizes our entrance to the kingdom of God and our new birth into His family.

Water baptism is not a means of salvation. Baptism in itself has no power to save. We are saved through faith in Christ (Ephesians 2:8, 9). Without this faith, the only thing baptism can do is get us wet. Still, we must not underestimate the importance of baptism as a sign of what happens to us when we are saved.

Water baptism is a death-and-life experience. It signifies both the death of our old self and the new life we have received in Christ. Submersion denotes the death of the person we used to be without Christ. The old life, built around my desires and me, is dead and buried (Romans 6:4). When we allow ourselves to be taken under, we let go of the old life, with all the sin that beset it. We recognize and affirm that this life is worthy of death and must be left behind.

But thank God that baptism does not end there. After death comes resurrection (Romans 6:5). To be raised up from the water denotes the birth of our new life in Christ. We leave behind the old life in order to take up the new. From now on we are dead to sin, but alive to God (Romans 6:10).

In baptism, we affirm our union with Christ. We are united with Christ in His death, and so we die unto sin. We are united with Christ in His resurrection, and so we live a new life unto God (Romans 6:11). Through baptism, we identify with Christ, declaring our faith in His death and resurrection and our experience of these things in our own lives.

WHY SHOULD WE BE BAPTIZED?

Baptism cannot save us, nor is it a requirement for salvation. Why, then, should we be baptized?

- Jesus voluntary submitted to baptism, though He had no need to. He serves as our example (Matthew 3:13-15).
- Jesus commanded that those who become His followers should be baptized (Matthew 29:19), and the apostles echoed this command (Acts 2:38).
- Water baptism is a testimony before God and before the world that we belong to Christ and His church. Baptism is a public affirmation that we have been welcomed into the family of God (Acts 2:41).
- Water baptism gives us the opportunity to enact the experience of what Christ has done for us, and it gives God the opportunity to affirm and reinforce its reality in our lives. Baptism can and should be an unforgettable spiritual experience, confirming our conversion and commitment to Christ.

WHO SHOULD BE BAPTIZED?

Baptism is not for infants, but rather for those who know what it means to sin and to repent of sin and find forgiveness through Christ. Those who are baptized should do so willingly, affirming their own decision to give their life to Christ.

Baptism is not just for those who have proved themselves "worthy" of it, nor is it only for those who have attained a certain level of Christian maturity. Baptism is a sign of faith and commitment. It should be one of our first acts of obedience as Christians, performed as soon as we can understand and assent to what we are doing (Acts 2:41). Everyone who believes in Christ should be baptized.

WHY DO WE CELEBRATE THE LORD'S SUPPER?

Jesus instituted the ordinance of the Lord's Supper on the night before His crucifixion. Sharing a final meal with His disciples, He spoke to them of His approaching death, and He used the bread and wine to symbolize the life He was offering as a sacrifice for them and for the world. In receiving the bread and wine, His disciples symbolically received the sacrifice of Christ and the life He laid down for them (Matthew 26:26-28; Mark 14:22-24).

In continuing to re-enact this ceremony of the bread and the wine, we remember that night and the holy and horrible events of the day that followed (1 Corinthians 11:26). Through the Lord's Supper, we proclaim and commemorate the sacrifice of Christ, and we affirm our own share in it.

WHAT DOES THE BREAD SYMBOLIZE?

The bread symbolizes the body of Christ (1 Corinthians 11:23, 24). Jesus called Himself the "bread of life," come down from heaven to give life to the world (John 6:48-51). Without Christ, we are spiritually dead, separated from the God who is the only source of life. God offers us His own glorious and eternal life to revive us, and we receive this life in Christ (1 John 5:11).

Receiving the bread of Communion represents receiving the life of God come down to earth in the body of Christ, offered to us in

Him. Eating the bread is the perfect symbol of our dependence upon Christ for our life. Our bodies need nourishment on a continual basis, and so do our spirits. We repeat the Lord's Supper regularly in acknowledgment of the fact that our spirits must continually feed on the life of Christ. As our souls feed on Christ, we are sustained spiritually, for He is our life.

Whenever you eat the bread of the Lord's Supper, remember that Christ's life is given to *you*. Jesus died, not only for the world, but also for you personally. He offers His life to you; receive it by faith.

WHAT DOES THE CUP SYMBOLIZE?

The cup of wine or juice symbolizes the blood of Christ, which purifies us from sin (1 John 1:7). In the Old Testament, the people of Israel celebrated the feast of Passover to commemorate the day they were spared from God's judgment and delivered from bondage in Egypt (Exodus 12). The people were told to put the blood of a lamb on their doorposts in order to protect their households from the angel of death. Jesus is the Lamb of God (John 1:29). His blood applied to our hearts saves us from God's judgment upon our sin, and it delivers us from bondage to it.

The blood of Jesus Christ sealed the new covenant He came to establish between God and humanity (Luke 22:20). This is the covenant of grace, under which God promises to forgive our sins and undertakes to redeem and purify us for Himself (Hebrews 8:7-12). When we drink from the cup, we renew this covenant before God, receiving God's offering of forgiveness and salvation and offering ourselves to Him in return. The Lord's Supper is a periodic remembrance and renewal of our covenant relationship with God.

Whenever you drink from the cup of Communion, remember that Jesus shed His blood—not just for the world, but also for *you* personally. Receive God's offer of grace, and offer Him your life in return.

HOW SHOULD WE CELEBRATE THE LORD'S SUPPER?

When we partake of the Lord's Supper, we must always do so in a reverent manner, remaining fully aware of the significance of what we are doing (1 Corinthians 11:27, 28). We must never treat lightly the elements that symbolize the body and blood of our Lord. We are to examine our hearts before we eat and drink, confessing our sins unto God in order to receive forgiveness and cleansing. In addition, we are to recognize and re-affirm our unity with the body of Christ in the local church and around the world, for we all share together in the life of Christ. If there are broken relationships among us in need of reconciliation, this is the time to seek and extend forgiveness.

Whether we partake of one loaf or individual wafers, whether we drink from a single chalice or from individual cups—the particular elements we use are not as important as the attitude of our hearts. The elements are material symbols of a spiritual reality, and they contain no magical power. However, when received with faith, they become more than symbols; they become channels through which God's grace and power flow to us. Taken in faith, they impart to us that which was contained in the body and blood of Christ: His very life.

REFLECT & RESPOND

1. What are the two ordinances Christ left the church to practice?

2. What is baptism and what is the significance of it for a Christian?

3. What is the Lord's Supper and what is the significance of it for a Christian?

Q&A

Read Romans 6:1-14.

1. What does water baptism symbolize?

2. Why is it important?

Read 1 Corinthians 11:23-32.

3. Why do we celebrate the Lord's Supper?

4. What does the bread symbolize?

5. What does the cup symbolize?

6. How should we partake of the Lord's Supper?

FOR FURTHER STUDY

Anyabwile, Thabiti M. and J. Ligon Duncan. *Baptism and the Lord's Supper.* Wheaton, IL: Crossway Books, 2011.

Schreiner, Thomas R. *Believer's Baptism: Sign of the New Covenant in Christ.* Nashville, TN: B & H Academic, 2007.

Schreiner, Thomas R. *The Lord's Supper: Remembering and Proclaiming Christ Until He Comes.* Nashville, TN: B & H Academic, 2011.

CHAPTER TEN:
God Is Worthy

WHO SHOULD WORSHIP GOD?

Everyone! God made all living creatures; all receive their life from Him, and all owe Him their worship (Psalm 150:6). Worship is a universal duty.

Of course, Christians have even more reason than others to worship the Lord (Psalm 107:1-3). Christians have greater knowledge of who God is and what He has done. God has not only created us, but He has redeemed us as well. He has given us not only life here and now, but also eternal life to enjoy Him forever. Therefore, we of all people ought to worship God.

One day all creatures will bow before the Lord and acknowledge His rule (Philippians 2:9-11). Even now, worship goes on continually in heaven (Revelation 4:8). But on earth, not everyone worships God. This makes our worship here and now of particular value to the Lord, for it takes place in a hostile environment. Thus, we now have a special opportunity to offer unto God a worship that is more precious because it is not universal.

WHEN SHOULD WE WORSHIP GOD?

Always! Worship is always appropriate, at any time of day or night (Psalm 34:1; Philippians 4:4).

Worship should be an everyday occurrence, not just a Sunday-only affair. Worship begins in our own private prayer time, when we come aside from the cares and duties of life to meet with our Father. It is there that we set the tone for the day—and for our lives. A daily time of devotion leads to a life of praise and worship.

Remember: Worship doesn't depend upon the circumstances. We are to praise God not only when things are going well, but also when they are not (Habakkuk 3:17, 18). Our circumstances may change, but God never does, and He is always worthy of our worship.

Similarly, worship doesn't depend upon our feelings. Worship is not something we do only when we feel like it. God doesn't change with our feelings, and neither should our worship. In fact, worship can be therapeutic; when we choose to offer the sacrifice of praise in spite of how we feel (Hebrews 13:15), we often find our feelings changing for the better.

WHERE SHOULD WE WORSHIP GOD?

Everywhere! Worship isn't just something that goes on inside a church building. Worship is a way of life, an attitude of praise that we carry with us wherever we go. Worship flows from our hearts at home, at work, driving in the car, shopping in the mall—anywhere. The whole world is God's sanctuary!

Nevertheless, having said this, we must recognize that there is something special about gathering with God's people for corporate worship. From the time of the ancient Israelites in the Old Testament, to the days of the early church in the New Testament, and throughout the centuries that followed, the people of God have made it a habit to meet regularly to worship Him together. This should be our practice as well (Hebrews 10:24, 25).

Individual worship is good, but corporate worship is better still. God's purpose is to make of believers a temple in which He can dwell (Ephesians 2:19-22). Thus, when we join together in worship, the presence of the Lord can be known and felt in a special way. Alone we are just single stones; together we form a holy temple, which can contain a greater measure of the glory of God.

The Lord takes special delight to see the hearts of His people united in worship and to hear their voices joined in exclaiming His praise. And we ourselves can find a foretaste of heaven when we come together with our brothers and sisters in Christ to rejoice in God, to tell and sing of what He has done for us. Worship is celebration! And when it comes to a celebration, the more the merrier!

WHY SHOULD WE WORSHIP GOD?

1. **God commands us to worship Him** (Psalm 150). Worship is a matter of obedience.
2. **God is worthy of our worship** (Revelation 4:11). He is to be praised for what He has done, His marvelous works of creation and redemption. And He is to be praised for who He is, Creator and Sovereign of the universe and Savior of His people.
3. **Worship has profound and beneficial effects on us.** In worship, we draw near to God and find a deeper sense of His presence (Psalm 100:4). Through worship, we come to see God more clearly and gain a better understanding of who He is (Psalm 48:1). As we worship God, our own problems fade into the background, and our perspective becomes clearer (Acts 4:23-31). Praising God strengthens our faith, as we focus on His greatness (Psalm 56:10, 11). Praise brings freedom, as we look at God rather than ourselves and let go of the things that bind us (Psalm 34:1-4). The Holy Spirit fills us when we praise and glorify God (Ephesians 5:18-20). As we focus on Christ in praise and worship, the Holy Spirit works to transform us into His likeness (2 Corinthians 3:18).

HOW SHOULD WE WORSHIP GOD?

By all possible means! We can praise the Lord in song and in dance, in drama and in music, through laughing and crying, shouting and praying, standing and kneeling (Psalm 150:3-5). Whatever we do, it should be done in accordance with Scripture. God has already told us how to express our love and worship to Him.

The way we choose to worship at a given time will depend upon where we are, our own particular tastes and talents, and what is on our heart. We may even worship the Lord in total silence, bowing before Him in quiet and reverent humility (Psalm 46:10).

According to Jesus, the important thing is that we worship God "in spirit and in truth" (John 4:24). What does this mean?

Worship God in spirit.

This means, first of all, that worship is a matter of the heart. The inward reality is much more important than the manner of the outward expression. No matter how loudly or skillfully we sing, play, or dance, it is all for naught if our hearts are not in it. True worship originates deep within our spirit, and then it comes forth in words and actions.

But to worship God in spirit also means to let the Holy Spirit direct our worship. The Holy Spirit is to be our guide in all things (John 16:13), and this includes worship. The Holy Spirit helps us in our weakness (Romans 8:26), and since the goal of His ministry is to exalt and glorify Christ, He is ready and willing to inspire and direct our worship.

On an individual level, the Holy Spirit first reveals within our hearts the reality of who God is and what He has done for us (1 Corinthians 2:9, 10), thus calling forth praise and thanksgiving in response. Then the Spirit helps to give expression to the praise in our hearts. He may lead us to shout, to sing, to laugh, to cry, or to dance. He may also give us words in an unknown tongue with which to praise God, words that go beyond the limits of our understanding in uttering what is in our hearts.

On a corporate level, the goal of Pentecostal worship is to allow the Holy Spirit to direct the praise of the whole congregation. We can think of the congregation as an orchestra, with the individual members as the musicians. The Holy Spirit inspires each musician to play a melody of praise, at the same time orchestrating the individual strains into a unified symphony of praise to God. When we allow the Holy Spirit to conduct our worship, the result is a beautiful harmony that gives a foretaste of worship in the new heaven and new earth.

Pentecostal worshipers are not passive spectators, but active participants. Pentecostal worship leaders seek the input of the Holy Spirit in everything from song selection to order of service to receiving the offering. They allow room for individuals to contribute to the service in song, prophecy, testimony, or speaking and interpreting tongues (1 Corinthians 14:26). At the same time, individuals must submit to the members of leadership, who are responsible for maintaining an orderly flow in the service (1 Corinthians 14:32, 33, 40). There must be a balance between freedom and order, for everything is to be done for the good of the church and the glory of God (1 Corinthians 14:26).

Worship God in truth.

This means, first of all, that our worship must be sincere, without hypocrisy. What comes forth from our lips should match what is in our hearts. We must open our hearts to God, not concealing anything or pretending to be something we are not, but coming to Him just as we are.

To worship God in truth also means to worship Him as He revealed Himself in the Bible. We must worship God in knowledge of who He truly is, not in a false idea of Him created from our own imagination.

Finally, to worship God in truth means to come to Him through Jesus Christ, who is *the* truth and *the* only way to God (John 14:6). We have access to God only through Christ. Our prayers, our songs, our offerings, our praise—everything we present to God—must be offered in the name of Christ.

WHAT IS WORSHIP?

We can think of worship as a three-step process:

1. Worship begins in recognition of who God is and what He has done for us, when our eyes are opened to see the truth about Him.
2. This understanding leads to thanksgiving and praise, as we begin to glorify God for His greatness and goodness to us.
3. Worship culminates in consecration, as we offer unto God not only our praise but also our very selves. The worship that begins in our hearts is not complete until we go on to offer our whole lives unto God as living sacrifices (Romans 12:1, 2).

Our lives are to be given unto God for Him to transform us and use us for His purposes. God wants the worship we express in local churches to spill over until it floods all areas of our lives, so that everything we are and do becomes an offering of praise to Him (Colossians 3:17). For God's people, worship is a way of life.

REFLECT & RESPOND

1. Worship of anything other than the one true God of the Bible is idolatry. What are some of the people, things, or ideas that people are drawn to worship rather than the one true God?

2. Why should we worship God?

3. Explain in your own words what it means to worship God in spirit and in truth. You may find Jesus' conversation with the Samaritan woman in John 4:1-26 helpful.

Q&A
Read Psalm 100.

1. According to the psalmist, who should worship the Lord?

2. How should we come into the presence of the Lord (v. 4)?

3. What kind of attitude should characterize our worship (vv. 2, 3)?

4. What are some ways to express our praise (vv. 1, 2)?

5. Why should we worship the Lord (vv. 3, 5)?

FOR FURTHER STUDY

Giglio, Louie. *The Air I Breathe: Worship as a Way of Life*. Colorado Springs, CO: Multnomah, 2006.

Keller, Timothy. *Counterfeit Gods: The Empty Promises of Money, Sex, and Power, and the Only Hope That Matters*. New York, NY: Dutton, 2009.

Tozer, A. W. *The Purpose of Man: Designed to Worship*. Ventura, CA: Regel, 2009.

CHAPTER ELEVEN:
God Gives

WHAT IS STEWARDSHIP?

The whole world and everything in it belongs to God (Psalm 24:1). This includes you and me and everything we possess. Our money and our time, our homes and our families, our bodies and our souls—God created them all, and they rightfully belong to Him.

God has entrusted these things to us to use and manage. They are only in our possession temporarily, and they pass out of our hands at death. But as long as we live, we are God's stewards, the servants He has put in charge of His property. We are responsible to manage what God has given us wisely and for His glory (Luke 19:13).

What does this mean? It means handling all our resources and possessions in the knowledge that we shall one day give an account of our stewardship (Matthew 18:23). This applies to everything we have. As stewards of our time, we are to use it productively and not waste it. As stewards of our bodies, we are to keep them healthy and not abuse them. As stewards of the earth, we are to take care of the environment and not despoil our natural resources.

The concept of stewardship applies with special force to our finances. The Bible has a great deal to say about the use of money and proper attitudes toward it. Knowing we must give an account to God for the way we handle our resources, we are expected to be honest in all our financial dealings. We are to avoid waste and extravagance.

And we should be generous in sharing with those who have less. We want God to be pleased with the way we earn and use the money He has entrusted to us.

ARE CHRISTIANS SUPPOSED TO BE RICH OR POOR?

Some people believe that God blesses those who are most deserving, or those who have the most faith. In their thinking, wealth is a sign of godliness. Others think that wealth is a sign of selfishness and that truly godly people will shun riches and embrace poverty. Both ways of thinking are mistaken. There is no virtue in either wealth or poverty. What really matters is not how much money we have, but how we acquired it and what we do with it.

Wealth often comes as a result of hard work and thrift, while poverty often follows laziness or wasteful spending (Proverbs 10:4). But such is not always the case in this sin-sick world. Wealth can be obtained through exploitation or dishonesty, and poverty may result from misfortune or injustice. In some societies, wealth and poverty depend primarily on which family a person is born into, and there is very little movement from one socioeconomic status to another. In short, it is a mistake to try to judge a person's moral or spiritual condition on their bank account.

Whether little or much, all that we possess comes from God (James 1:17), and we should be thankful for what we have (1 Timothy 6:8). Those who have an abundance should be grateful for God's blessing. But with greater wealth comes greater responsibility (Luke 12:48). The more we have, the more we must give account for.

Both wealth and poverty bring temptations that test us in different ways (Proverbs 30:8, 9). The poor are tempted to envy the rich and to complain against God. The wealthy are tempted to accumulate possessions for self-centered purposes (Luke 12:20, 21) and to trust in their riches instead of God (1 Timothy 6:17). Of the two, wealth appears to bring with it the greatest temptation to sin (Matthew 19:24; 1 Timothy 6:9). Jesus recognized its power over us, and He warned us severely against allowing it to steal our loyalty and affection away from God (Matthew 6:24).

Perhaps the poor are more likely to recognize their dependence upon God and to thank Him for their daily bread. On the other hand, those who are wealthy have great opportunity to be channels through which God can bless others. They have the privilege of sharing with those in need, and they are able to use their wealth for the furtherance of the kingdom of God (1 Timothy 6:18, 19).

WHAT IS TITHING?

Tithing is the practice of giving ten percent of our income back to God. The tithe is first mentioned in Scripture with Abraham, then later with Jacob. These patriarchs of the faith offered a tithe of what they received in acknowledgement that it was God who had blessed them and as a token of gratitude to Him (Genesis 14:18-20; 28:20-22).

When Moses presented the laws of God to the people of Israel, tithing was established as a mandatory practice (Leviticus 27:30). God claimed for Himself a tenth of the produce of every field and flock, and He commanded the Israelites to return it to Him. Failing to give God the tithe that was due Him was considered stealing from God (Malachi 3:8, 9).

SHOULD WE PRACTICE TITHING TODAY?

Although the Mosaic law which commands tithing no longer binds us, there are nevertheless good reasons for us to continue the practice:

1. Our reason for tithing is the same as that of Abraham and the nation of Israel: to acknowledge that all we have has come from God's hand. Tithing is one way we can express both our gratitude for what we have received and our faith that God will continue to supply our needs (2 Corinthians 9:12).
2. While Jesus criticizes the legalistic Pharisees for emphasizing scrupulous tithing over the weightier matters of justice and the love of God, He nevertheless affirms tithing as a commendable practice (Luke 11:42).

3. God blesses those who tithe to support His work or mission (Malachi 3:10; Luke 6:38; Acts 20:35).
4. Having received the grace of God in Jesus Christ ought to compel us to give cheerfully and generously (2 Corinthians 8:7-9; 9:7).

WHERE SHOULD WE GIVE OUR MONEY?

It is neither necessary nor possible to give our money directly to God, so it is given to His representatives, to those who minister in His name. In the Old Testament, the tithe was brought to the temple—the place of worship—and shared with the priests and Levites who carried on the work of the temple. In the same way, today we bring our tithe to the local church where we worship.

There are many godly and effective para-church organizations that are worthy of support. But our first obligation is to the local church to which we belong. God instructs us to give financial support to those who give us spiritual nourishment (1 Corinthians 9:13, 14). The tithe should be given to support the pastor and ministries of the local church.

The local church is made up of individuals who are committed to Christ and to one another. An important part of this commitment is financial. The local church depends on its members for support; it has no other source of revenue. We cannot claim to be truly a part of the church if we are withholding from it our financial resources.

WHAT ABOUT OTHER OFFERINGS?

The tithe should be seen as a starting place. Of course, we cannot give what we do not have, but most Christians in affluent nations can and should give more. Our giving should be in proportion to what the Lord has given us, and it should be a reflection of the gratitude we feel in our hearts (2 Corinthians 8:12). Our offerings should be seen as tokens of our love to God.

The offerings we give over and above the tithe may be given wherever we please, though we ought to make sure they are used wisely and for worthy causes. The local church will often have special needs or projects, and we will likely find other ministries, as well, to which we will want to contribute. The Scripture mentions two areas of ministry in particular to which every Christian (and church) ought to give:

Missions

Christ commissioned His church to proclaim the gospel to every people group (Matthew 28:19), and those who do not go have an obligation to support those who do (Romans 10:14, 15). The task of world missions is the responsibility of every Christian. And what better use for our money than in spreading the gospel?

The Poor

Time and again the Bible admonishes those who have to share with those who have not (Leviticus 19:10; 1 John 3:17). Indeed, God promises to repay those who give to the poor (Proverbs 19:17), for He views what we give to the poor as gifts unto Him (Matthew 25:40). We must never forget our responsibility to the poor, for it is only by God's grace that we do not find ourselves among them.

We should not settle for giving only what we can spare. If our giving is not a sacrifice, then it is worth little (2 Samuel 24:24). Yet we will never really suffer for what we give, for the more we give, the more we will receive (Luke 6:38).

We should not view giving as a burden or duty, but as an opportunity. We are blessed to be able to invest our money in God's mission and to reap eternal rewards from what we give in this life (Matthew 6:19-21).

ARE OUR MOTIVES FOR GIVING IMPORTANT?

More important in God's sight than how much we give is *why* we give. God is interested in the attitude with which we give, and He looks at what is in the heart as well as what is in the offering plate.

Jesus emphasized that our giving should never be done to impress others, and He recommended anonymous giving for this reason (Matthew 6:2-4). Neither should we give grudgingly or reluctantly, but we should give only because we really want to give (2 Corinthians 9:7).

Giving should come naturally to Christians because we have received so much (Matthew 10:8). God's people are generous because God is generous.

God wants us to give cheerfully, joyfully, and out of an overflowing heart. We give out of love: love for God, love for our fellow believers, love for those in need, and love for the lost. God gave His best in order to demonstrate His love for us (John 3:16). In the same way, giving is a great way to demonstrate *our* love as well.

Just as the ancient Hebrews brought gifts to the temple to worship God, the offerings we present should be an integral part of our worship. Indeed, we should never forget: giving is worship too.

REFLECT & RESPOND

1. What is stewardship and why is it important for the Christian to practice stewardship?

2. Where are we supposed to give and use our resources (time, money, abilities, etc.)?

3. How should Christians use their resources (time, money, abilities, etc.)?

Q&A
Read Luke 12:13-34.

1. Does the quality of our life depend upon how much we possess (vv. 15, 23)? Why or why not?

2. In the parable, why did God call the rich man a fool?

3. Do you think God can be trusted to supply your material needs?

4. Which is more secure, treasure on earth or treasure in heaven?

5. What or who is to be our treasure? Where is your heart?

FOR FURTHER STUDY

Alcorn, Randy. *The Treasure Principle: Discovering the Secret of Joyful Giving*. Colorado Springs, CO: Multnomah, 2001.

Piper, John. *Don't Waste Your Life*. Wheaton, IL: Crossway Books, 2007.

Stott, John. *The Grace of Giving: Ten Principles of Christian Giving*. Peabody, MA: Hendrickson, 2012.

CHAPTER TWELVE:
God Sends

After Jesus' resurrection from the dead and before He ascended into heaven, He gave this command to His disciples:

> All authority in heaven and on earth has been given to me. Therefore go and make disciples of all nations, baptizing them in the name of the Father and of the Son and of the Holy Spirit, and teaching them to obey everything I have commanded you. And surely I am with you always, to the very end of the age (Matthew 28:18-20).

This passage is sometimes called the "Great Commission," for with these words Christ commissioned His followers with the task of making disciples of all people groups. The church has taken these instructions as its marching orders ever since.

WHO IS SUPPOSED TO CARRY OUT THE GREAT COMMISSION?

Jesus gave the Great Commission to His eleven disciples. But obviously Jesus did not intend for these eleven men to travel throughout the world and carry out His instructions on their own. No, this mandate was given to *all* followers of Jesus, from the first generation down to our own day. We are also His disciples, and the burden of explaining the gospel to the lost rests upon us as well.

The word *evangelize* means "to tell the good news." The gospel is the good news of the coming of Christ; His death, resurrection, and ascension; and the forgiveness, redemption, and new life He offers to all who believe. God has not written the message of salvation in huge letters across the sky, nor has He assigned to angels the task of communicating it to a lost humanity. God has ordained that those God has saved through hearing the gospel share it with others.

Evangelism is not just something professional preachers do. All who have received salvation in Christ have the privilege and responsibility of sharing what they have received with others. We do not all do this in the same way; our abilities and opportunities differ. But whether to large crowds or to individuals, whether speaking, writing, singing or passing out gospel tracts, all of us can find some way to share the good news.

WHEN SHOULD WE SHARE THE GOSPEL WITH OTHERS?

The gospel is not just for Sundays. Today is the day of salvation (2 Corinthians 6:2). We should always be prepared to share the gospel with those around us (1 Peter 3:15): at home, on the job, wherever we may be. This does not mean that we make ourselves obnoxious, preaching at everyone we meet. Rather, we stay alert to the opportunities that God brings our way, and we willingly share with any who show an interest (Colossians 4:5, 6). We must learn to act and speak with wisdom, never compromising the truth of the gospel, but taking care not to become a stumbling block ourselves.

WHAT IS THE NATURE OF OUR TASK?

Scripture employs several useful images to help us understand the nature of our task.

Ambassadors

Paul says that we are *ambassadors* for Christ (2 Corinthians 5:20). An ambassador is a person who represents someone else, speaking and acting on behalf of another. God has assigned us the role of His ambassadors, entrusting us with the message He wants the world to hear. We are to tell people that God loves them and that, through Christ, He has made a way for their broken relationship with Him to be restored. As divine representatives, we deliver this message with the full authority of God Himself. We are to reach out to people on His behalf, urging them to come to the God who loves them more than they know.

Witnesses

Jesus said that we are to be His *witnesses* (Acts 1:8). A witness is someone who has personal knowledge that he can share with those who do not. A witness is called upon to tell what he has seen and heard (Acts 4:20). We are to tell others what Christ has done for us, how we have experienced His love and grace in our lives. Like John the Baptist (John 1:7), we testify to who Jesus is, the crucified Savior and resurrected Lord.

To explore the courtroom metaphor further: it is helpful to realize that we are not prosecutors, tasked with convicting people of sin; we are not defense attorneys, tasked with explaining and justifying the ways of God or the state of the church; we are not judges, tasked with rendering a final verdict on the lives of people; we are witnesses, tasked with telling "the truth, the whole truth, and nothing but the truth," as we know it.

Light

Jesus also referred to His followers as the "light of the world" (Matthew 5:14). Jesus brought the light of God into the world, shining with holiness and glory (Hebrews 1:3). But with His return to heaven, the church is left to shine in His place. What we do and say are to show the world what Christ is like. Our attitudes and actions should display something of the holiness and love of God (Matthew 5:16). The light of Christ is to be reflected in the lives of His people. In this way, we shine the light of God's truth and glory into the darkness of a wicked world (Philippians 2:15).

Salt

Jesus also called His followers the "salt of the earth" (Matthew 5:13). The world we live in is under the judgment of God (John 3:19), and it is headed for destruction (2 Peter 3:10). But just as salt serves as a preservative, keeping meat and fish from going bad, so our influence can restrain the evil in the world and thereby hold back the judgment of God (Genesis 18:26). Through words of truth and acts of righteousness, Christians can exercise a positive influence on society and culture and make the world a better place. However, in order to be effective agents of preservation, we must be careful not to lose our distinctiveness as Christians (Matthew 5:13). It is only in living differently from the world that we can be of benefit to it.

HOW CAN WE ACCOMPLISH OUR TASK?

To present and represent Christ to the world is indeed a high calling. Who is equal to such a task (2 Corinthians 2:15, 16)? But God has not left us to our own devices. The Holy Spirit provides the wisdom and power we need to explain the gospel effectively and to live out the reality of it. Jesus said that the Holy Spirit would make us His witnesses (Acts 1:8). His words proved true in the lives of the apostles, and the same Spirit will work effectually in us. We must learn to depend upon Him to lead us in what to say, to give us strength to proclaim the truth boldly, and to trust Him with the results.

We cannot save anyone. Only Christ can save, and only the Holy Spirit can lead a person to faith. Our part is to be faithful and truthful in declaring the gospel and to live a life that will confirm the truth of what we say (2 Corinthians 6:3). We do not need to engage in emotional manipulation or try to impress anyone with eloquent speech (1 Corinthians 2:1). Our confidence is not in our skills and abilities, but in the truth of the gospel and its power to save (Romans 1:16).

Sharing the gospel is a simple matter of speaking the truth in love (Ephesians 4:15). To this end, we should learn to explain the gospel clearly and understandably, and we must show love and respect to those we seek to bring to Christ. May the Holy Spirit equip us to do this, and may He use us to lead others into the family of God.

WHAT IS THE SCOPE OF OUR RESPONSIBILITY?

We have seen that the Great Commission has been given to the whole church and that evangelism is the responsibility of every Christian. This responsibility encompasses three areas:

1. **Personal Contacts.** On an individual level, we are to bear witness to our family and friends, our colleagues and classmates. These are often the most difficult to talk to, but those who know us best are likely to be more influenced by what they see in our lives than what they hear us say.

2. **Local Community.** As part of the local church, we should be engaged in regular forms of outreach to our community or city. Every local church is to be a lighthouse beaming forth the gospel, shining the glory of Christ in the midst of the surrounding darkness. The church is to make a priority of multiplying believers, praying and working to reach the lost in the immediate area. We must join in and do our part, using our gifts to help in any way we can with revivals, crusades, concerts, visitation, etc., and striving to make our church a place where people can meet God.

3. **The Nations.** There is no nation, tribe, or ethnic group that doesn't need to hear God's message of salvation. The gospel of Christ is for everyone, and God intends for this gospel to be preached throughout the whole world (Matthew 24:14). Ever since its beginning, the church has sent forth messengers to take the gospel to people who have never heard it (Acts 13:3). Down through the centuries, these missionaries have willingly left their families and homelands, endured hardship and opposition, and even risked their lives to tell the world about Christ.

But missions is not just the responsibility of missionaries. The task is too large and important to leave to just a few. Taking the gospel into the whole world is the responsibility of the entire church, and every believer has a part to play, a job to do (Romans 10:13-15). Missions is a partnership between those who go and those who send (Philippians 1:3-5). Those who send play a vital role in praying for the missionaries and the lost they are trying to reach and in providing the funds to support their ministry. What role does God have for you? Will you be a goer or a sender?

Every Christian should be a witness for Christ. Every Christian should help the local church with the task of evangelizing the local community. And every Christian should be involved in world missions. Little or much, we can all do something to help see the Great Commission fulfilled. What will you do?

REFLECT & RESPOND

1. What is the gospel? What are Christians to do with this message?

2. With whom should we be looking for opportunities to actively explain the gospel?

3. Do you have difficulty sharing the gospel with some people more than others? Why? Ask the Holy Spirit for boldness to overcome your fear.

Q&A

Read 1 Corinthians 1:18-25.

1. Can the world know God through wisdom? How can it know Him?

2. Will everyone accept the message of the gospel?

3. Some demand miracles or logical proof to establish God's existence. How does Paul respond to such demands?

4. Why does Paul refer to Christ as the "power of God" and the "wisdom of God"?

FOR FURTHER STUDY

Coleman, Robert E. *The Master's Way of Personal Evangelism.* Wheaton, IL: Crossway Books, 1997.

Piper, John. *Let the Nations Be Glad: The Supremacy of God in Missions.* 3rd ed. Grand Rapids, MI: Baker Academic, 2010.

Platt, David. *Radical Together: Unleashing the People of God for the Purpose of God.* Colorado Springs, CO: Multnomah, 2011.

CHAPTER THIRTEEN:
God Returns

IS JESUS COMING BACK AGAIN?

Just as surely as Jesus came into the world roughly 2000 years ago, He will return someday. His second coming is as certain as His first. But how do we know Jesus is coming back again?

- Jesus promised to return (Matthew 26:64).
- Jesus often spoke of His return in parable and exhortation, urging His disciples to be ready for that day (see Matthew chapters 24, 25).
- The apostles taught that Jesus would return (Acts 3:19-21).
- Angels testified that Jesus would return (Acts 1:11).
- The return of Christ is a prominent theme of the whole New Testament, and it has been the blessed hope of believers from the first days of the church to the present (Titus 2:13).

HOW WILL JESUS COME BACK?

The second coming of Christ will be like the first in that He will return literally and bodily, not just in some spiritual or symbolic sense (Acts 1:11). He will come back in the same glorified physical body in which He was resurrected and ascended into heaven.

The second coming of Christ will differ from the first in several important ways though:

- Jesus came the first time to begin the process of redeeming this fallen world; He will come the second time to complete the process (Romans 8:19-23).
- The primary focus of Jesus' first coming was salvation; the primary focus of His second coming will be judgment (Acts 17:31).
- Jesus came the first time as the suffering Lamb, offering no resistance to His enemies; He will come the second time as the conquering Lion, destroying His enemies with the breath of His mouth (2 Thessalonians 2:8).
- Jesus came the first time in humility and meekness, His glory hidden from view; He will come the second time in overwhelming splendor, His glory shining forth like the sun itself (Luke 21:27). The second coming is referred to in Scripture as the "revelation" or "unveiling" of Christ, for then He will be seen as He is (1 John 3:2).

WHEN WILL JESUS COME AGAIN?

No one knows when Jesus will return (Matthew 24:36). Jesus warned us time and again that His return would come as a surprise, that there would be no way of knowing the time of His coming (Matthew 24:44; 1 Thessalonians 5:1-3).

Nevertheless, people have persisted in trying to predict what Jesus said could not be known. Over the years many declared that He would return on this date or that, and always they have been proved wrong. It is difficult to say who is more foolish, those who make such predictions or those who believe them.

It is futile to try to guess the date of Christ's return. God hid this information from us for a purpose: He wants us to be ready at all times (Luke 12:40).

Certainly Jesus' return will come as a surprise to those who do not know Him and so do not expect Him. It should not be a surprise to us. This is not because we know the date of His return, but because we are always watching, always waiting for Him (1 Thessalonians 5:4, 6). We are to be ready whenever He comes.

WHAT SHOULD BE OUR ATTITUDE TOWARD THE RETURN OF CHRIST?

The return of Christ is the foundation and anchor of our hope as Christians. We do not feel at home in this world, for we know it is not as it should be; persecution and frustration, evil and injustice are ever present. God's people are looking for a kingdom where righteousness and peace reign always (Isaiah 42:1). We seek a permanent home (Hebrews 13:14) that we can share with our loved ones, beyond the reach of death's cruel intrusion (Revelation 21:4). We desire to replace these diseased and decaying bodies with glorious, immortal ones (Philippians 3:20, 21). We long to see with our own eyes the one who gave Himself for us (1 Peter 1:8). When Christ the King returns, all our hopes will be fulfilled because all our hope is found in Him.

The promise of Christ's return teaches us to hold loosely to the things we have here and to value things differently than the world does. We know that the political and social structures of this present age are temporary and that the glorious and eternal kingdom of Christ could replace the kingdoms of this world any day. We recognize the higher value of what is unseen but eternal, and we resist the temptation to seek after the fleeting pleasures and fading prizes this world offers (2 Corinthians 4:18). We don't worry about piling up assets here, for we won't possess our real treasure until Jesus, our treasure, appears (Matthew 6:19-21).

The impending return of Christ does not mean we need do nothing but sit back and wait for Him. The second coming is no excuse for idleness (2 Thessalonians 3:6). Neither should we allow curiosity to breed an unhealthy fascination with end times, so that we spend all our time trying to figure out the exact schedule of events for things to come. On the contrary, knowing that our Lord may come back any day spurs us on to work harder than ever for Him, so that we may accomplish as much as possible before our opportunity is gone (Luke 19:13).

Knowing that Christ may return tomorrow does not mean we need not plan for the future. After all, He may not return for another thousand years. Therefore, we must live prudently, watching for Him to come today, planning in case He does not. Of course, all our plans are made tentatively, in submission to the will of the Lord (James 4:13-15). The important thing is to be faithful and obedient so that whenever He does come, He will find us working faithfully at our appointed tasks (Luke 12:37, 38).

The promised return of Christ gives us no license to plunder the natural world or to mistreat our own bodies. The old creation will not be totally destroyed, but it will be redeemed and renewed. Our renewed life will be lived in glorified bodies in the new heaven and earth. It matters how we treat our bodies and the earth we inhabit (Romans 8:19-23), for we are stewards of both. Expecting Christ to return, we are motivated to live holy, godly lives (2 Peter 3:11-14). We strive to live righteously and blamelessly, for we want Him to be pleased with us when He comes (2 Timothy 4:7, 8).

WHAT ARE THE SIGNS OF CHRIST'S COMING?

When His disciples asked Him about the signs of His return, Jesus warned them not to be deceived by what would happen in the years to come: wars, natural disasters, persecution, and the appearance of false messiahs (Matthew 24). All these things have occurred, and we can expect them to continue. We are not to be alarmed at such things (Matthew 24:4-6), for they are typical of life in this fallen world. Jesus said that life will go on normally until the day of His coming, and it will surprise most of the world (Matthew 24:37-39).

We do know that these last days will be difficult and dangerous (2 Timothy 3:1). But they will also be days of widespread preaching of the gospel (Matthew 24:14). Those who optimistically believe that scientific or social progress will lead to some kind of utopia on earth will be sorely disappointed. The only thing that will save this world from destruction is the return of Christ (Matthew 24:22). But no matter how bad things get, the people of God need not fear, for we are assured of our destiny in Christ (1 Thessalonians 5:9).

WHAT WILL HAPPEN WHEN CHRIST RETURNS?

The Great Tribulation

At the time of the end, God will cease restraining the lawlessness that even now wreaks so much destruction in the world. A strong leader will arise who will set himself up in the place of God and gather behind him the forces of evil, both human and demonic (2 Thessalonians 2:3-12). They will persecute the people of God, and many will be martyred or lose their faith (Matthew 24:9-12). At this time, God will begin to pour out His wrath upon this rebellious world (Revelation 16:1).

The Uniting of Christ With His Church

Christ will come to take His bride, and the Church will be caught up to be united with Him (1 Thessalonians 4:16, 17). Christians who have died will be resurrected into new, glorified bodies, and the believers who are living will be transformed without seeing death. All this will happen in a split second, as we are changed from mortal to immortal and pass from decay to glory (1 Corinthians 15:51-53).

The Final Judgment

In the end, all who remain in rebellion against God, whether devils or human beings, will be defeated and destroyed. All the unbelieving dead will be raised to life to face judgment before the throne of God. All will be judged according to what they have done and will suffer the punishment they deserve in hell (Revelation 20:11-15).

The New Heaven and New Earth

God will complete the redemption of His fallen creation, refashioning a new heaven and earth where all the ravages of sin are no more—no pain, no sorrow, no death (Revelation 21:1-4). We will spend eternity exploring the glories of God's new creation, enjoying the fellowship of our brothers and sisters in Christ, and savoring the presence of God among us (Revelation 22:3-5). It will be our eternal delight to worship and serve the Lord together in a world filled with the knowledge of the glory of God (Habakkuk 2:14). Now we can only begin to imagine all that God has in store for us, but we will have all eternity to find out (1 Corinthians 2:9).

Even so, come, Lord Jesus!

REFLECT & RESPOND

1. How will Jesus come back?

2. Is it important that Jesus will return? Why? How should it impact your everyday life?

3. What will Jesus do when He returns?

Q&A
Read Matthew 25:14-30.

1. In what way are we like the servants in the parable?

2. What kind of Master do we have?

3. What does God expect us to do while we wait for Jesus to return?

4. What do you think it means to "hide the Master's money"?

FOR FURTHER STUDY

Clouse, Robert G. *The Meaning of the Millennium: Four Views.* Downers Grove, IL: IVP Academic, 1977.

Erickson, Millard J. *A Basic Guide to Eschatology: Making Sense of the Millennium.* Revised. Grand Rapids, MI: Baker Books, 1998.

Morgan, Christopher W. ed. *Is Hell for Real or Does Everyone Go to Heaven?* Grand Rapids, MI: Zondervan, 2011.

ABOUT THE AUTHOR

Russell Board and his wife, Sandra, have served as missionaries for over 27 years in France, Italy, and most recently in Japan since 1989. He is the continental director for Asia and the Pacific for World Missions Ministries of the International Pentecostal Holiness Church.